Bert Widman

Why, Paul ?

An evolutionary inquiry.

In plain language.

In Paulum

O. A. M. D. G.

LIST OF CONTENTS

****

Introduction, Part I

They usually came at four in the morning. At that time, they knew, the families would be exhausted from keeping vigil on the roofs and would succumb to a short sleep. At that time also the streets would be empty and no onlookers could disturb the proceedings with shouted questions. So if the raid was carried out with surprise, speed and no undue sentimental questions, it would be successful.

Successful also this time. The platoon of soldiers advanced cautiously in the narrow lane of mud-walled houses, the moon painting tell-tale reflections on their metal helmets. Their helmeted leader conferred shortly with a figure clad in an ankle-low mantle before an iron gate of a one-storied house. Then he whispered a short command at his platoon: over the wall, without a sound !

Which they did, forming robbers'ladders with hands and shoulders for their comrades. Once inside, they watched their platoon commander to give the agreed signal: to push up his fist. It came. Within a split second the small courtyard of the house erupted in pandemonium. With shrill cries the soldiers banged at the doors and windows of the house with their weapons, a detail of three went to work on the house door with a crowbar.

Their calculated cries were met instantly by real shrieks of fear and desperation inside the house. The psychology of it was, this the soldiers had been trained to, that their wild cries would stifle any organized opposition within the house, even if it had been planned. The inhabitants would not have time to organize flight or resistance in this ear-splitting ruckus.

So it was. When the door came crashing out of its hinges the soldiers could stop to make their mock battle cries because all the noise came now from the unlucky inhabitants, in mortal fear and utter desperation. The grown-ups knew what was coming to them. The children, of course, did not, therefore they screeched loudest.

They clambered to the women, hiding their heads in the garments of mother, aunt or grandmother. The elder children were wide-eyed and paralyzed with fear.

The man, father, husband, still drowsy from a few minutes of sleep, scarcely felt the leather strings that were cutting into his wrists. He only added to the melee with his eruptive shouts of No! Please! No! Not my children! No! Not my wife! Have mercy!

When the soldiers pushed them out of the house with the butt of their weapons they hissed: Quiet! Or we shall kill your children! This worked, as they knew from other sorties. Father and mother suffocated in pain and tears but kept their mouths shut in order to preserve the children.

Which, of course, was a ruse. After the parents had been marched off out of sight, the children who were able to walk were collected also, their tiny wrists tied behind their backs, as their parents went.

One boy, on this occasion, was not collected by the militia, he was simply overlooked in the uproar. But when he saw his mother being dragged out of the house and beaten by the soldiers, the young boy of seven ran after them and flung himself between his mother and the soldier. The sandal that hit him mid-face and broke his nose, however, was not the soldier's.

It was the hit of the commissar of the platoon who was watching the whole proceedings from the house gate, enveloped in his long cloak. For good measure he kicked the sprawled body of the child carefully with all force in the temple of the head and went after the departing platoon.

When the marching steps and the wailing of the victims had dropped out of earshot, the heads on the neighbouring roofs came up from their hidings:
„Have you seen this? Isn't it horrible?"
„It was the Temple Guard. Probably our neighbours were members of this new sect that proclaims the crucified Yeshua as the Messiah!"
„What will our Synhedrium do with them?"
„Men and women will be flagellated and, if they do not recant, will be stoned to death before the city gate".
„I think Pilate reserved capital punishment for his court?"
„Not any more after the trial of this Yeshua. He realized that no bribes could be exacted, so he left it to the Synhedrium to issue death verdicts in matters of faith".
„And the children of these couples?"
„Will be sold into slavery".
„Who was that man in the long cloak who watched all this from the outside?"
„This is Saulus. He has been put in charge of all these operations. He really is after their blood. May God have mercy on them!"

****

Introduction, Part II

If I would speak with the tongues of men and angels
and had no love
I would be a sounding brass or a tinkling cymbal
And if I had the gift of prophecy
and knew all mysteries and had all knowledge
and if I had a faith that I could remove mountains
and had no love: I am nothing.
And if I would give all my goods to the poor
and give my body to be burned
and have no love
I would reap no profit.
Love suffers long and is kind, knows no envy.
She does not vaunt herself, is not puffed up;
she is not ambitious, seeks not her own,
is not irritated and does not think evil.
She does not rejoice over iniquity, but over truth.
She suffers, believes, hopes and endures all.
She never ceases to be.

Paul the apostle, Cor. I, XIII.

1 With all due respect

When my friend Walter and I wrote down our basic discussions in the little book „The Stone Age of Faith“ there was not the time or place to discuss the letters of Paul under an evolutionary aspect. We decided that Paul should receive a clear analysis of his own. This is the content of this book. Please listen to us as we designed our approach:

B: The so-called christian churches and their spin-offs point to Paul of Tarsus, a city which still exists under its old name near the Mediterranean coast of southern Turkey, and they venerate him as a canonized saint of the first order and as the chief architect of their belief -

W: Why architect? Would not chief ideologue be a more suitable title?

B: I see no difference in these labels. He really constructed a house of faith in which the christians of Hebrew, Greek and Roman tradition should live together. This will remain his major historical achievement.

W: All so-called christian churches and most of the sects pride themselves that their present state has largely been shaped by the doctrines of Paul. Quite obviously they are not aware of the bitter irony of their praise. Of course they are right, because also the seed of their present agony had been planted in Paul's teachings. The German writer Heine once remarked that without him the christian faith would be just another Jewish heresy today, non-existant in fact.

B: This is a nice bonmot but it does not stand up to the evolutionary view. If there had been no Paul then there would have been other carriers of the belief. The whole process would have been much slower probably but would have surfaced internationally also in the course of generations. The revelation through Yeshua is, and was ment to be, contagious.

To say therefore that nascent Christianity owes ist survival to Paul means that there was never another option - a definitely non-evolutionary view. We have come to know today that evolution never puts her eggs in one basket only.

W: But he was chosen by the Spirit who talked from Yeshua, or by the transfigured Yeshua itself - not himself - thank you!

B: Credo quia absurdum - I believe him because this decision from above is so utterly absurd to our minds.

W: If we believe Paul in that then we have to acknowledge also that he talked and wrote in the Holy Spirit, isn't it?

B: Objection! Massive objection! For once Paul himself was not quite sure whether he wrote in this enlightened state. He took it for granted sometimes, in other rare moments of modesty he surmised it only. *)

---

*) For the convenience of the reader the citations from Paul`s letters or other sources are given at the end of each section. The wording of the King James bible was upheld, although checked against the Vulgata text.

(B): Secondly I doubt this on the grounds of the evolutionary analysis to which we are subjecting his views in our book here, where the jury is still out.
Thirdly I object to it because the contention is a shield only which the spiritually beleaguered young christian church hastily planted before Paul's teachings in order to stop - and persecute - any criticism of them.

W: Were the letters ever canonized by a Council? I cannot remember to have read it?

B: There was no need to do so for a long time. When - as later in Islam - the oral tradition had produced unending garlands of pious fiction, up to approximatelxy 180 A.C., the search for reliable written material set in.
In the first line the four reports on Yeshua were considered to be authentic by tacit consensus, and likewise most letters of the apostles, with Paul all of them, for the simple reason that much more was not available that connected directly to the roots, except some apocryphal texts which went lost largely.

Since the strained dialectics of Paul seemed to outclass the simple and straightforward style of Mark, Matthew and Luke there developed immediately the situation which Hans Christian Andersen described in his fable „The King's new robes“. Nobody but Peter admitted publicly that Paul's writings are dark and hard to understand, for fear of being viewed as non-enlightened. The same was and is true for some German philosophers whose „unfathomable deepness“ is largely due to the fact that they shunned precise speech.

(B): So there was hardly any need for Paul's letters to be granted the highest status by a council; he was considered singular from the very beginning. All so-called Fathers of the Church had already paid homage to him long before the first council convened.

W: The higher bible criticism that has set in since the last century gives Paul an unusually harsh treatment. Some of the letters are deemed not come from his hand. Linguists have done comparative post mortems on syntax and vocabulary used within each letter and have come to the conclusion that the secretaries of Paul sometimes gave their own impressions. Psychologists maintain that the diction of Paul is governed often by excess mental strain with possible bouts of epilepsy. All these findings are credible. The pious rage which Paul developed when explainings the basics of the new creed to Festus pervades practically all his letters. So if all this is true, what is the use of our evolutionary approach to his texts?

B: My answer is that if I stick a revolver in your belly and tell you to surrender, would you ask me first whether there is a real bullet in the barrel or a blank cartridge only?

W: I suppose not. Why are you asking that?

B: Because the so-called christian churches have held a gun to the consciousness of their believers for 1.900 years with Paul's teachings and nobody dared to ask whether the cartridges were blanks or not. They were believed to be"live" and very much so. It does not matter, therefore, what was really in them, but what people were made to believe they contained. Seen this way it does not matter at all whether his letters were truly written in the Holy Spirit or not, or whether parts were written by eager secretaries who dared not to admit that they could not follow the torrent that was gushing forth from Paul. It is of no consequence either whether Paul was suffering from attacks of epilepsy. The essential fact is that for 1.900 years the God-inspired and infallible status of his writings was „under the gun" and whoever contested this did so at the peril of his life.

W: I do not think that the example of the gun is very enlightening, my friend. There was no need for it anyway because the unholy pact between secular powers and church organizations was soon working perfectly, based on the questionable marriage which Paul had prepared for them.

B: It does not matter who is holding the gun, or firing the stakes. The churches and the ordained powers of the old world acted in beautiful collusion, at least until the medieval popes developed their delusions of grandeur.

W: But also Augustine, Thomas Aquinas and Luther did not feel under the spiritual gun, quite to the contrary. For them Paul was the welcome quarry from which they could mine the building blocks of their doctrines -

B: - not to forget Calvin with his - rather, Paul's - merciless predestination!

W: Exactly, and it was a very convenient quarry. Because the letters of Paul have so many long-drawn sentences, rattling with empty word shells and being compounded by a tautology where anything is the proof of everything, it was relatively easy to ferret out exactly those building blocks that supported the particular prejudice.

B: So we are running this risk also in the analysis we are going to do?

W: I do not think so. If we were looking for building material that would support the evolutionary view of the revelation through Yeshua then there would be no book probably, because we know already that these glimpses are very rare indeed in his writings. No, on the contrary: we are going to show how Paul stands in the way of an evolutionary understanding or believing of the revelation. So, no quarry for us.

B: I agree. When we were discussing Paul in recent years we said that he had planted totem poles on the way to the better understanding of the Spirit through Yeshua. Before each of these totem poles we feel the grip of Paul's hand in our neck, trying to press you down until your nose touches ground in reverence. And only then you are freed to march on - to the next pole. Da capo.
So what we are going to do in our book is, speaking profanely and clearly, to fell totem poles, right?

W: Basically yes. If the reader has studied the list of contents carefully he/she has seen that we are going about it methodically and selectively. Otherwise we could create the impression that we are attacking Paul indiscriminately. This is not the intention. What we want to show is that certain major concepts of his are still rooted in the Stone Age, hindering a trusting and joyful acceptance of the revelation and effectively barring the evolution of consciousness of half the world's population for more than 1.900 years.

B: Stop here, please! I do not agree with this outline. The way you say it it sounds as if we were trying to drag Paul before the High Court of Evolution and accusing him of having sabotaged spiritual evolution on our planet for a considerable span of time. In other words we are accusing him under a law that we realized only some 150 years ago, of which people who lived 1.900 years before us had no notion whatsoever. A classic tenet of jurisdiction forbids to employ a law against a perpetrator that was promulgated after his deed. In our case this means that Paul cannot be held responsible for having slowed down the train of evolution because evolution as such was simply not known to him. He preached and wrote on the given knowledge and understanding of his time.

W: Stop now! Stop! You are bringing in the famous defense line now which the so-called christian churches and sects are applying each time when the contents of speeches or writings of their protagonists clash with reason or humanitarian issues. No, they say, our man/woman has to be seen in the „historical context", meaning that any interpretation has to consider the historical background and framework of thought at his/her time.

(W): No objection so far. If somebody writes philosophy or religious texts in his/her „historical context“ we take them at face value, but only if they are not violating human rights - and most of them do. This filter can be upheld to anybody and in any century within the past 1.900 years since the revelation through Yeshua. But still - they are registered with us as personalities of their time.

But now we are coming to the point: anybody who is proclaiming or only assuming that he acts in the Holy Spirit must be measured as to what positive contribution towards the evolution of consciousness he/she has made, far over and above the „historical context“. If the result is nil, or negative, then the cooperation with a Divine Spirit simply did not occur.

B: Are we showing this in Paul's letters?

W: Yes. The reader may decide for himself/herself after having read the last chapter of this book. If commanded truths are pushed aside then everybody under his/her free will is entitled to a personal view on Paul. This must be respected at all times. And in this respect, before Paul the man and before the free will of the reader, we start our book.

Quotations having a bearing on Section 1:

Quotation	Source
.... and I think also that I have the Spirit of God	Cor I, VII, 40
And as he thus spoke and gave reason Festus cut in loudly: Your are mad, Paul! This much learning leads you into madness!	Acts XXVI, 24

2 The exterminator

W: We are meeting Paul, or Saul at that time, in the Acts as the precursor of future inquisitors, SS and NKWD henchmen.
He was approximately 20 to 25 years old at that time. His youth and mercilessness plus probably the recommendation of his teacher Gamaliel won him the appointment as the anti-heretics commissar of the Synhedrium.

B: Every time I read those lines I get physically sick of this monster. The fanaticism which stayed with him for life was fired in his Saulus era by the so-called Old Testament which was blood-thirsty as ever also, or especially, against heretics. If three reliable witnesses testified that „they had served other gods“, these heretics were to be led outside the city gates and to be „stoned with stones until they die“.

W: Worse still, this insane fury was dictated to your next of kin.
„If your brother .... or your son or your daughter, or your dearest wife or your friend who is nearest to your soul are whispering to you secretly“ let us go and serve other gods ...“ you shall not consent nor listen to them; neither shall your eye have pity on them, neither you shall ... conceal them. You will be sure to kill them.

B: And for good measure: „You shall not suffer a witch to live.“
In these texts we are having the roots of all later witch hunts and Autodafés, acts of faith, as the burning of heretics was semantically camouflaged.

W: Was Saul a mass murderer?

B: Objectively yes, also in his own retrospect of later years, but without ever using the word „murder“.

W: Do you think that he enjoyed the torture to which men and women were subjected before they were handed their death sentence?

B: Yes, he later revealed his active participation in a side remark.

W: Do you think that his perverted attitude towards women was a result of his sadism?

B: No, this was cemented already in his mind by the so-called Old Testament. But in his warped mind I think he felt the same perverted pleasure as did Dominican inquisitors much later when a beautiful female body was stretched on the rack.

W: If this should be so then he was worse than all the nazi or communist henchmen; most of them simply liquidated people, effectively and without inner turmoil.

B: So it is. I think he is the most detestable person on whom we have reports of these times. He is nauseating me.

W: More detestable than the Judas who sold the information on Yeshua's nightly whereabouts to the Synhedrium?

B: Definitely. Judas had lost faith in Yeshua or in the Spirit talking from him, that was his driving force. But he had no pleasure in torturing or killing people. His remorseful suicide is speaking for him.

W: Saul had a wonderful excuse later, when he was Paul: all his manifest acts of cruelty were practically dictated to him by his zealous defense of the true religion.

B: This is not an excuse, only an explanation of motive. With the same reasoning the butcher Alba washed his hands over the massacres in the Netherlands or a French king over a Bartholomew's Night, down to all the miserable creatures who were willing and profiting denunciators, judges and henchmen of the inquisition.

W: Acting on higher orders was the standard defense argument of the Nazi elite who stood trial in Nuremberg after World War II, and of all concentration camp commanders. Also in the case of Saul these orders were quite from this world, from the Synhedrium. Saulus apparently volunteered to be the executing commissar. Gamaliel was sure to see his seed blossom now in this young firebrand.

B: And no word any more from Nicodemus?

W: None. Either he kept silent or was silenced. We do not know.

B: So if this Saul had not been put in charge of the persecution campaign somebody else would have been put in command, right?

W: Of course. But the criminal energy which Saul instantly developed, fired also by a profile neurosis, left no doubt that nobody was suited better for this task than he.

B: We have read the Acts and the letters of the converted Saul carefully and no literature we studied came harder on us. What we were looking for invain was an unconditional plea for mercy and forgiveness by the man who called himself Paul now. The Acts are using already the detached language of a historian, in more or less the same way as we are looking back on inquisition times. Small wonder, because they were written by his disciple Luke who did not want to be a muckraker or insult his patron. So all the bloodcurdling misery, pain, torture of fathers and mothers, the suffering of their children and the brutality of stoning to death dozens, if not hundreds „heretics" under Saul's supervision was very quickly and tidily swept under the carpet of history.

W: Public memory is a short-lived commodity, as younger history confirms. Take Joseph Fouché, one of the commissars of the French revolution regime. He made piecemeal of hundreds of „counter-revolutionaries" in Lyon by artillery shrapnel and yet went on to become police minister first under Napoleon and, small surprise, also under the Bourbons. Everybody knew that the later Duke of Otranto was a mass murderer, but everybody kept his mouth shut, for good reason.

B: The silencer in our case was an authority that even Peter could not dismiss, who hated the very guts of Saul/Paul: the transfigured Yeshua, now called the Christ. We have already said in the aforegoing section that this reversal is so totally non-understandable to us that its very absurdity seems to be the proof of its authenticity. This Christ knew that the same tempestous zeal, intolerance and dedication would now be harnessed to the trail-blazing of the new faith, which it did.

W: The same Christ, if we accept this event, must have been aware also that Paul, as we are calling him now, was firmly rooted in the Hebrew dogmatic belief and that he would use the so-called Old Testament as the basis for his preaching of the saviour of this world.

B: Of course, what else? All apostles inclusively Peter, excluding perhaps John, had no other basis for their arguments than their 2.000 year old Hebrew theocratical system.

W: Paul learned to speak the Greek language. Did he come also into contact with the Greek philosophers?

B: I doubt that very much. As long as he was Saul, certainly not. Growing up in an ultra-orthodox Hebrew household he never even had an inkling of their works. Later, when he was confronted with them on his mission travels in the Mediterranean theatre he had only disdain for them. I doubt very much that he read one opus of Platon or Aristotle to the end.

W: What matters to us and the reader is not this, but something else:
apparently the Divine Spirit forgave Saul the murderer, transforming him into a weapon for his purposes. Do we also forgive him or not?

B: What you meant to say really is that we cannot put ourselves above God, right?
So I am saying simply: secundum contritionem ejus - to the extent that he really and deeply repented. If he did so, then it was not reported to us in a believable way.

W: Isn't the life he started into as Paul, which certainly was anything but joyful, not one drawn-out act of repentence, plus his beheading?

B: This is the doctrine of the so-called christian churches, I know.
Paul kept statistics on the forms of the numerous crimes inflicted on him; one may certainly see it this way. Personally however, I do not believe that Paul understood the following years as a protracted martyrium in order to wash away the blood from his hands. I think that the now unfolding activities, setbacks and successes were the challenge to the basically unchanged fanatic temperament of Paul which he needed and used on a worthy target now.

Repentance? One single word of it, unconditional and not rationalized away by a „zeal for the religion of my fathers" would have been much more credible to me. But apparently the new creed could not use self-depreciation because it could have been misinterpreted as a weakness. So, if it really happened, Luke and/or the scribes of his letters saw to it that the dead remained dead.

W: Give me an honest answer now: we both dislike Saul, but do you like Paul?

B: No.

W: Do you think that this is a fair basis then for our discussions in the next sections?

B: Yes. You must not share my opinions. We are in a dialog, remember?

Cited texts in Section 2:

Quotation	**Source**
And at that time there was a great persecution against the church which was at Jerusalem; and they were all scattered abroad throughout the regions of Judaea and Samaria, except the apostles. .... As for Saul, he made havoc of the church, entering into the houses and hauling men and women and committed them to prison	Acts, VII, 58-59 Acts, VIII, 1-4
- as quoted on page ... -	Deut. XVII, 25
- as quoted on page ... -	Deut. XIII, 1-9
- as quoted on page ... -	Exod. XXII, 18
And I said: Lord, they know that I imprisoned them and beat in every synagogue those who believed in you	Acts, XXII, 19

Quotation	Source
Which thing I also did in Jerusalem; and many of the saints did I shut up in prison, having received authority from the chief priests. And when they were put to death I gave my voice against them. And I punished them often in all synagogues and compelled them to blaspheme. And being exceedingly mad against them I persecuted them even unto strange cities	Acts XXVI, 10-12
For you have heard of my conversation in time past in the Jews'religion, how that beyond measure I persecuted the church of God and wasted it. And profited in the Jews'religion above many my equals in mine own nation, being more exceedingly zealous of the traditions of my fathers	Gal. I, 13-14
(I) who was before a blasphemer and a persecutor and injurious: but I obtained mercy because I did it ignorantly in unbelief	Tim I, I, 13-14

Quotation	Source
Beware lest any man spoil you through philosophy and vain deceit after the tradition of men, after the rudiments of the world	Col II, 8
Perverse disputings of men of corrupt minds, and destitute of the truth, who think to ask questions is piety, from such withdraw yourself	Tim I, VI, 5

3 Collective guilt, final atonement

B: Over the centuries the theocratic state of the Hebrews passed one law after another similar to nets with an ever decreasing width of mesh so that even the smallest fish could not slip through. Finally, at Paul's time, they arrived at Law no. 613 and only their priests and upper caste were able to keep track of them.

W: Where there is no law there is no sin; in reverse: where there are many laws the probability of man to sin against them is not increasing in a linear trend, but in an exponential curve, because of the intrinsic domino effect. The violation of one rule invariably produced scratches on others as well - an inescapable system.

B: Paul saw this very clearly. But instead of attributing to their leading castes the juridical morass of intransigence, fanaticism and disdain of humanitarian values the whole network was God-inspired for him. Outside of this canon there existed no moral law, as he told the non-Hebrews in his letters repeatedly.

W: It appears only logical that under such a codex the numbers of trespasses per annum was enormous; because of this the high priest loaded the sins of the people each year symbolically unto the famous scapegoat, poor animal, and shooed it into the desert. What was not resolved, however, was the origin of sin. Reading backwards in their scripts this was not hard to find however, the first time that a human will turned against or neglected the will of God: Eve and Adam, she in the first place of course.

B: Deplorable as this stone age view is, it could be swallowed as an example setting incidence. But the Jews needed an explanation for negative occurrences and developments under the exclusive treaty with their deity: why was this Jahve mostly angry with them and ditched them finally, instead of promoting them to world dominance, as prophesied? All the sins committed against him, therefore, must have sprung from a poisoned well - the primordial sin of Adam who was a historical figure for them. Since they were descendents of Adam this guilt was inexorably passed on into all their generations; each newborn carried the invisible stigma of this guilt.

W: I would not have minded this superstition very much if it had been confined to their masochist ideology. But the Hebrews maintained, and so did Paul naturally, that the whole world became guilty before their God, since Adam was not only their forefather but the first man on earth! The guilt could be only collective, therefore.

B: In their eye-for-eye mentality also this first sin must have had immediate consequences; not only the expulsion from a garden Eden but, from now on, death for all human beings with delayed resurrection until the end of times.

W: This last tenet, of course, went straight against the central teaching of Paul, because he hinged his whole message on the resurrection of Yeshua. There was no other way out of this dilemma than to pronounce Yeshua to be the first man who rose from death; in fact it was he who abolished death as an enemy of man, invented by the sheitan.

B: There this unsavory circle closes. I have no difficulty to believe that the Jews - turned - Christians accepted this theory without question, because one half of the circle had been their precious belief already. I am surprised, however, about the docility of the non-Jewish christians to whom this tribal belief was fed. We read, of course, in the letters of Paul in repeated instances his warnings of false teachers, without specification, and of his curses against them. Could it be that the non-Jewish christians rebelled against their commanded inclusion into this guilt-atonement circle of a culture that was foreign and barbaric to them?

W: It would be a good explanation since the message reached not only the slaves and low castes but also those who knew their Democrit, Platon and Aristotle.

B: I think that we have explained the glacis sufficiently. Now it is high time that we disagree, isn't it? I am starting:
If the Holy Spirit had really been with or in Paul's consciousness it would have told him a few facts, namely:

- First, that Adam never existed. Therefore, no primordial, least of all collective guilt;

- secondly, that Israel is not representing the world;

- thirdly, that the Divine Spirit whom the Jews degraded to a Jahve cannot be insulted by man, has no plans for revenge or demands for collective atonement, therefore;

(B): - Point four: no reconciliation by Yeshua was necessary; his murder was the logical end of his fight against the fossilized system;

- Point five: the immolation of his own „son" makes a caricature of any deity: no earthly sacrifice appears worthy or potent enough to wash away the sins of the world; only the insulted deity itself must be slaughtered in a human body in order to forgive the world -

W: Would you stop now, please? It is very easy to pass judgement on Paul from our remote point of view. Of course all these points are valid, as we have said in our previous book. The problem Paul had to face, however, was to connect his message of Christ to an already existing basis of faith -

B: Sorry for interrupting you, but this is exactly the point where the whole edifice of faith that Paul erected was based on quicksand! For once, his non-Jewish listeners had no need of a Hebrew tribal history. Not so, says Paul, upholding the primate of the Hebrews to be the exclusive owners of this revelation first, which was handed down to the non-Jews only after Israel had snubbed it, but still in its totality.

Secondly, and this is far more important: there was no inherent need at all to connect the necessity of the revelation to a tribal history, because it was addressed to the whole planet and not to roughly 1 per cent of its population. The Holy Spirit was and is very much aware of this, I think, in every habitat where the revelation appears. So what would have hindered it to realize in Paul the urge to make a clean break with Jewish history, especially with the unbearable notion of primordial sin? Can you tell me?

W: I think I can. For once, Paul would have been the enemy of two parties: the Synhedrium and the followers of Yeshua who were very much rooted in the Jewish belief. On the other hand such a break would hardly be in consonance with evolution, which, as we know today, „non facit saltus" - makes no jumps - but occurs always in variations or mutations of orders that offer themselves as a suitable basis -

B: I beg your pardon!! Do you really mean to say that a clean break with Jewish superstition, tribal history and fanatical intransigence would have resulted in the end of christian belief before it ever could get started?

W: Exactly. In my opinion the Divine Spirit foresaw this risk clearly and avoided the confrontation or invasion of Paul's consciousness on purpose.

B: I have to control myself very much not to shout at you! What you are saying is nothing less than, counting roughly from the year 100 A.C., 1.900 terrestrial years could go by with all their blood and tears resulting from a stone age of faith because it was better to have a misguided mutation than none at all? Are you still in your senses?

W: I think I am, thank you. What surprises me really is that you have apparently given up to believe in evolution. There is no instant evolution. There is no instant new religion. The God which Yeshua was preaching the Jews was hardly recognizable for them any more, an enormous mutation, already in itself, if you so want it, but it still connected to the 2.000 years of their belief.

The Pharisees and Sadducees knew very acutely that Yeshua kept telling them that they had no idea of the God to whom they paid lip and law service; but still they never could accuse him to preach a new deity - for which the penalty would have been instant.

B: So you mean that there was no chance for Paul either to preach a clearly changed deity?

W: He had not the slightest intention to do so because the idea as such did not occur to him, nor was it implanted into his consciousness by a Holy Spirit. He used the Jewish platform without any second thoughts, exept for the circumcision which he spared the non-Jewish christians. And therefore this platform exists in all so-called christian churches and sects up to our days as a commanded basis of faith. That it would tie down the belief in the revelation by a stone age of faith was clearly foreseen by Markion already, who was quickly silenced as a heretic, however.

B: Are you of the opinion, that only now, in our days, the evolution of consciousness on our planet has prepared a new platform of thought from which we can waive good-bye finally to all the ballast of the so-called Old Testament without endangering the revelation?

W: This is what I think, yes. The quantum leaps in natural sciences, be it the inquiry into the last particles of matter or into the remotest parts of the universe have made it possible that we can change also our concept of the Divine Spirit - something which was not open to Luther. And you will agree with me that 2.000 terrestrial years is but a mere half second to evolution.

B: This truth is always very loftily said and does not fail to make its impression in print or speech. I do not share this detached view, my friend. I look back on 1.900 years of

(B): spiritual and bodily terror which the so-called christian churches and their sects worked on this planet, as long as they had an awe-inspiring Jahve in the background - or foreground. I know that it is futile to do such post mortems. On the other hand every effort must be made now to correct this development decisively.

W: Thank you for this word. I also think that we are in for a decisive mutation, but only now, not in the times of Paul.

Original texts having a bearing on Section 3:

Quotation	**Source**
Wherefore as by one man sin entered into the world, and death by sin; and so death passed upon all men, for that all have sinned .... death reigned from Adam to Moses, even over them that had not sinned	Rom V, 12-15
Therefore as by the offence of one judgement came upon all men to condemnation; evenso by the rightousness of one came the justification to live upon all men. For as by one man's disobedience many were made sinners, so by the obedience of one shall many be made righteous.	Rom V, 18-20
.... for by the law comes the knowledge of sin	Rom III, 20
.... for you have been bought at a high price	Cor I, VI, 20
So Christ was once offered to bear the sins of many	Hebr IX, 28

Quotation	Soure
For as many as have sinned without law shall also perish without law; and as many have sinned in the law shall be judged by the law	Rom II, 12
.... raised up Jesus our Lord from the dead, who was delivered for our offences and was raised again for our justification	Rom IV, 25
For since by a man came death, by a man came also the resurrection of the dead	Cor I, XV, 21
.... Jesus Christ, who gave himself for our sins, that he might deliver us from this present evil world	Gal I, 4
.... Jesus who delivered us from the wrath to come	Thess I, I, 10

Quotation	Source
For all have sinned and come short of the glory of God. Being justified without merit by his grace through the redemption that is in Christ Jesus. Whom God has set forth to be a propitiation through faith in his blood, to declare his righteousness for the remission of sins that are past, through the forebearance of God, to show his justice in our times, that he might be just and the justifier of whomever who believes in Jesus.	Rom III, 23-25
And wherefore has Christ, when we were still weak, in due time died for the ungodly?	Rom V, 6
Much more then, being now justified by his blood, we shall be saved from wrath through him.	Rom V, 9
For the wages of sin is death; but the grace of God is eternal life in Jesus Christ our Lord.	Rom VI, 23

Quotation	Source
.... because we thus judge, that if one died for all, all then all were dead	Cor II, V, 14
And all things are of God who has reconciled us to himself through Christ and has given to us the task of reconciliation. To wit, that God was in Christ, reconciling the world unto himself, not confronting them with their sins, and has put in us word of reconciliation.	Cor II, V, 18
.... that he might deliver us from this present evil world, according to the will of God, our Father	Gal I, 4
And, having made peace through the blood of his cross, by him to reconcile all things unto himself	Col I, 20
And you, who you were once alienated and enemies in your mind by wicked works, he has reconciled you now in the body of his flesh by death	Col I, 21-22

4 The stench of blood

W: Do you think it was wise to choose this caption?

B: Maybe it is not very polite but it brings the issue into an immediate focus: we are confronted with atavistic concepts about the value of ritually spilled blood, especially that of human beings. The early Hebrew tribal history does not report sacrificial killings of prisoners of war as it has come to us in gory detail from the Aztecs, for instance. But we are not very far off the mark, I think, if we say that we are not putting it beyond them. The last-second intervention from above towards an Abraham who was dutifully going to butcher his beloved son is seen - allegorically today - as the end of human sacrifices in general in this ethnic group.

W: And so they turned to animals as substitutes?

B: This is the general view. The new practice made it also possible for the priest caste to recycle pieces to their private households free of charge.

W: But the blood had to go out before, as it still is commanded today with kosher meat?

B: In a desert climate this makes hygienic sense, just as the circumcision of the male penis, sure.

W: But the sacrificial blood was considered to be something special. If sprinkled by the priests, or even the high priest, it had both spiritual cleansing power and was a renewal of the covenant which the Hebrews had concluded with their deity.

B: Very much so since the time when they smeared their doorposts in Egypt with it so that the angel of death would not strike against them by error - for everybody who subscribes to this story.

W: Can't we say that the Hebrews considered blood to be the most precious liquid they knew and valued it higher, therefore, than water for instance?

B: Of course. Otherwise the sprinkling of it over the heads of the believers and over the whole inner sanctum of their temple cannot be understood. In these instances it was „holy" blood which carried atonement and forgiveness in one.

W: And as this totem it was handed down over generations until Paul saw the singular chance to connect the blood spilling from Yeshua's lacerated body to arrive at this barbaric instrument of salvation, right?

B: So it is. He erected this totem pole for all believers in the new creed, of course also for the non-Jewish followers. For the Jewish apostles who were brought up in this tradition, also for Peter, this was a matter-of-fact constituent of the revelation which needed neither interpretation nor an extra blessing from their side.

W: So another totem pole could be raised that said that the redemption of this world - see our aforegoing section - could be effected only because the blood of Yeshua dripped to this earth - cleansing it from all sin and preserving it from the wrath of God. Correct?

B: Alas, it is correct. It is like being transported back into the Stone Age. Something I cannot understand, however, is that later sharp minds, also Luther, were not repelled by the stench of blood that rises from Paul's letters?

W: Why should they? Once you accept that a human body has to be sacrificed, that of Yeshua, blood is part of the happening. The atavistic Hebrew links to a sacrificial blood transported this notion smoothly into Christian belief as preached by Paul. And there it is still today.

B: Paul was not consistent, however. The Hebrew religion detested any contact with crucified humans, cursed them in fact. Not so, however, with the body of Yeshua?

W: This is easy to explain, because Paul was quick to give the cross a new salvation identity of its own, but only since Yeshua had been nailed to it. He made a point of preaching the crucified Christ.

B: And the resurrected one, not to forget. But I share your view that not the appearance of the saviour of this world and his „eu-angelion", the good and joyous acceptance of the revelation were the center-point of his teaching but the proof that damnation from this world had been lifted only because of Yeshua's torture, death, and above all - blood.

W: In my opinion he exchanged an atavistic guilt complex for a more subtle one. The crucified Christ had repaid a mortgage that the Hebrew deity had slapped unto the whole world - I can utter this monstrosity each time with difficulty only - but substituted it at the same time with the debt of gratitude that - again this whole world - owes to Yeshua now.

We said in the aforegoing section that anybody who raised doubts on the necessity to redeem the world was flirting with death, until some 400 years ago. The guilt complex that Paul introduced in his doctrine has simply changed the creditor; formerly it was Jahve, now it is Yeshua the Christ.

B: Sacrificial blood is the name of the totem pole before which we are standing. What shall we do with it?

W: Put the axe to it, what else? I hope it is coming down with a crash that is duly heard!

B: Now, now! Let's not become emotional! If my mind were completely unbiased, which it is definitely not, I would say that we are saying farewell to a fossil of faith that is comparatively easy to dismantle because its stone age origin is manifest. But it is not that easy for me. The bloodshed by Yeshua is considered in the so-called christian churches and sects to be „the" decisive event in their whole pageant of salvation.

In my opinion the over-use of the word „blood", especially by Paul but also by others, has helped to lower the barrier for bloodshed in general during the past 1.900 years of throat-cutting over religious disagreements.

(B): On the other hand the orthodox believers of nowadays read over these lines with scarcely a shrug because they are so much used to this vocabulary that the vulgarity of it is not screaming in their faces, as it should do every time.

W: It is definitely easier to clean a slaughterhouse than scripts that are a commanded part of faith. But if these churches throw out the blood then the whole string of collective guilt/final atonement is inextricably sticking to it. So it must be ruptured out with it, isn't it?

B: If they would allow evolution to enter, this would consequently happen. But they don't. They are feeling very smug in their room of faith with tightly closed windows, unaware that the stench of blood is a major ingredient of the toxic waste they are inhaling.
As we said: asphyxiation.

W: Why is it so hard to push open a window and let fresh air into this room?

B: Because the neatly stacked documents of faith would be scattered around, or get lost. And not only those reeking of blood.

W: Have you noticed that none of us has voiced a dissenting opinion in this section?

B: I realized it and I do not like it at all. But apparently our vista is congruent for a change, why not?

Original texts that have a bearing on the contents of Section 4

Quotation	Source
.... much more then, being now justified by his blood, we shall be saved from the wrath through him	Rom V, 10
.... but now in Christ Jesus you who sometimes were far (from God) are made near to him by the blood of Christ	Eph, II, 13
.... who has delivered us from the power of darkness and has translated us into the kingdom of his dear Son, in whom we have redemption through his blood, even the forgiveness of sins	Col I, 14
.... and, having made peace through the blood of his cross, by him to reconcile all things unto himself	Col I, 21

Quotation	Source
.... (Christ, the high priest) .... neither by the blood of goats and calves, but by his own blood he entered into the holy place (tabernacle) having obtained eternal redemption for us	Heb IX, 12
Whereupon neither the first testament was dedicated without blood. For when Moses had spoken every precept to all the people according to the law, he took the blood of calves and goats, with water and scarlet wool, and hysop, and sprinkled both the book and all people, saying: this is the blood of the testament which God has enjoined unto you. Moreover he sprinkled with blood both the tabernacle and all the vessels of the ministry. And almost all things are by the law purged with blood; and without shedding of blood there is no remission	Heb IX, 18-22
Having, therefore, brethren, the trust to enter into the holiest by the blood of Jesus	Heb X, 20

Quotation	Source
.... of how much sorer punishment, suppose you, shall he be thought worthy, who has trodden under foot the Son of God and has counted the blood of the covenant an unholy thing, wherewith he was sanctified?	Heb X, 29
.... wherefore Jesus also, that he might sanctify the people with his own blood, suffered before the (city) gate	Heb XIII, 13
Now the God of peace that brought again from the dead our Lord Jesus, that great Shepherd of the sheep, through the blood of his everylasting covenant	Heb XIII, 21
.... and having made peace through the blood of his cross, by him to reconcile all things unto himself	Col I, 20
.... through sanctification of the Spirit, unto obedience and sprinkling of the blood of Jesus Christ: Grace unto you and spreading peace	Ep.Petri, I, 2
.... and the blood of Jesus Christ his Son cleans us from all sin	Ep. Joannis I, 8

5 The Cross

W: The cross certainly is the most successful logo of all history. Is it because of its simplicity or because of its indiscriminate use over the centuries? What emotions are we feeling when we are using this word?

B: Two thirds of the population of this planet see in it the trademark of religions or sects whose God was nailed to a wooden cross some 2.000 years ago like any other criminal. What is not understood, however, is the contention of these organizations that the blood spilled on this one cross has saved the whole world from an act of vengeance by an irate deity.

Having taken note of this, their interest in this gore-spilling religion ceases automatically mostly.

W: To be condemned to death on the cross was an insult added to terminal injury; its was reserved for the punishment of capital crimes, including lese-majesté and other offences against the ruling system. It was working long before the death of Yeshua and long after.

B: When the Romans finally conquered Spartacus and his ex-slave army they nailed their prisoners to roughly 6.000 crosses that were erected along the Via Appia from Capua to Rome - the year was 71 B.C.

W: I think that just as much timber was used in those times for these killing instruments than for shipbuilding.

B: Enough. We see Yeshua dying, and relatively fast at that in contrast to the usual protracted period of suffering. His blood trickled from the beams in small scarlet rivulets. Exitus.

Paul, however, saw something quite different before his spiritual eye. He saw the cross with the corpse of Yeshua projected high over this world and a light shining from it that enveloped the earth in a brilliant shine of divine forgiveness, for all sins past and those to come. Before Paul the cross was merely an execution instrument; for him it was an instrument of salvation, intrinsically connected to the personality of Yeshua so that not only the „Son of God" was transfigured for all future but also the idea of the Cross.

Had he read Platon he would have found a due place for the idea, which Platon puts before the thing. Paul, however, made a totem pole of it, carrying all the insignia of an absolute faith with no room for tolerance, humanitarian values, least of all love. Bow before it or be damned is the - sometimes verbatim - request in his scripts.

W: I said in the beginning that the cross became a logo. People are identifying, associating things with a logo. What associations were intended by Paul?

B: Submission first of all, as I said. Then the dire warning that before meriting the everlasting life any believer has to suffer in this world, following the example of Yeshua.

(B): For me this is one of the most incredible and unnatural tenets of him. Since he was subject to persecution, dangers and illnesses it seemed only fair to him that his believers should be exposed to their share of tribulation as well before entering the kingdom of God. The idea that entry could be allowed also to those who, by luck, were not smitten never entered his mind.

W: Was this the reason why the cross - abstracted - became also the synonym of human suffering?

B: Only within the so-called christian organizations. Just think of the islamic countries who refused the idea to join the International Society of the Red Cross. They had seen enough of it during the crusades and under the Reconquista. So they founded their Red Crescent instead, a very consequent decision in my opinion.

W: I feel that the cross - christian version - has been misused over the centuries on a grand scale from army banners down to the Iron Cross which Hitler wore as his World War I decoration. I wonder why the Vatican State never choose the cross as its symbol?

B: Because they picked one which signifies much more power: the crossed keys, locking or unlocking eternity, as the Spirit in Yeshua allegedly told Peter.

W: Helena, mother of emperor Constantin, was able to find the true cross on which Yeshua had died. Any comments?

B: If it is true or not, it is completely irrelevant for the revelation through Yeshua. 100 years after the alleged find so many churches and abbeys boasted to own a splinter of the „true“ cross that quite a number of originals could have been built from them. This is all besides the point. The hard fact is that the cross had not only been given a new identity by Paul but almost a co-personality to his Christ, whom he did not want to see otherwise than in his last stage of obedience on this earth: on the cross. This is why he took this morose pride in preaching Yeshua The Crucified, as he is underlining in his texts. Why not the living, preaching one?

W: I feel how you are regretting the fact that the sun is not shining in Paul's mind; he was unable apparently to cherish the good and natural gifts of this earth. The cross that he has erected throws ist dark shadow over all bodily or spiritual joy which this world is able to offer - because the world in itself is governed by the sheitan, of course, and all her splendour is worked only to distract the minds of people from God's stern demands. Happiness and cross do not mix, and the cross has preference because Christ hung on one. This is Paul's simplistic, atrocious philosophy.

Have you ever felt an elation while reading his letters? Do you find a smile here and there, perhaps a little humour? None of that. His left forefinger is pointing up to the cross, his right forefinger is poking at you, telling you to obey his doctrine which is spiked with contradictions, ideas of divine vengeance, damnation and curses for the non-believers, detest for philosophy, warnings of amoral women, hate of human flesh in every form - that is Paul's message of the cross.

(W): Reading more than three pages of him makes me feeling depressed. How was it possible that one person was able to let the whole joy evaporate from the revelation? Apparently he felt well in his mental mausoleum, but I certainly do not, you do not, nobody does, if he/she is honest enough to admit it.

B: I do not. But again our discussion lacks some salt, don't you think? I tried to find openings for dissenting ideas, but I have to admit that I found none because I share your views fully.

W: So what should happen? Should the cross be abolished and substituted by the silhouette of a dangling noose? Or a guillotine?

B: The true believers will rip you into fine pieces, literally, if you say that in public. You better never try it. The reason is that the cross has become „holy", a taboo which you must not touch if you love your life. Nobody would trade arguments with you or discuss Paul's sinister attitude towards it - no! They would simply shut you up at once in every legal or criminal way. And this is the deplorable effect that Paul has wrought among terrified and vaccillating minds over generations, that the cross is standing today for orthodox and litteral belief in the revelation through Yeshua and that no other interpretation is possible, necessary, nor wanted. That is the crux of the cross.

W: So what do we do?

B: Outwardly nothing. But I see the splinters flying already where my axe is biting into the totem pole.

Original texts that have a bearing on Section 5

Quotation	Source
For the preaching of the cross is a foolishness to those that perish, but unto those who are going to be saved, this is we, it is the power of God.	Cor I, I, 18
Because the Jews want to have signs and the Greek seek wisdom; but we preach the crucified Christ, a stumbling block to the Jews and unto the Greeks a foolishness.	ibd. 23
Christ has redeemd us from the curse of the law, being made a curse for us; for it is written: Cursed is everyone who hangs from the wood.	Gal III, 13
And I, brethren, if I yet preach circumcision, why do I suffer persecution? Because the stumbling block of the cross has vanished.	idb. V, 11
.... and that he might reconcile both unto God in one body by the cross	Eph II, 16

Quotation	Source
.... and having made peace through the blood of his cross, by him to reconcile all things unto himself	Col I, 20
.... he humbled himself and became obedient unto death, even the death of the cross	Phil II, 8

6 Enemy no. 1 : body and sex

B: Since Paul the so-called christian churches and sects have an abdominal problem, or rather: they prefer that an abdomen does not exist in the belief in God and that there is no problem, therefore.

W: We have a chameleon totem pole before us. With most lines of Paul the body, whom he likes to call „the flesh“, is the villain that is producing sin. One has to ask whether Paul never was told of Yeshua's famous dictum that whatever enters or leaves the body naturally is never evil. Only what leaves an evil mind is evil. And there we are directly back to Paul.

I maintain that in all matters of body, flesh and sex he had an evil, sometimes downright leering mind. But then come the chameleon changes: a few lines afterwards he reminds his followers that their bodies are temples of the Spirit. And again, on another occasion he sighs that in himself, his flesh, dwells no good thing.

B: I think that without being a psychiatrist it is not very farfetched to say that one of the major reasons of Paul's hate-love for the body, especially for the female body, is the primitive dualism he developed: the body, by its very „nature“, is against God. Only castigation and keeping a sanitary distance to (female) bodies can keep the enemy down - but not permanently, as he very well knows. This dualism is practically pervading all his teachings every time the subject comes up -

W: - and it comes up more often than any other points he tries to make. Obviously he was aware that his armour was full of holes in this issue. Otherwise he would not have seen the need to press the case against body and sex so often and so explicitly.

Sometimes the exhortations seem to be written with an expert eye, e.g. when he takes great care to warn his disciple Timotheus of the sexy charms that young widows are radiating; apparently this was the most dangerous group - by experience maybe?

B: A certain love of detail is noticeable also in some other instances, e.g. when he is informing the Romans about homosexual love - of both men and women - in Greece.

W: Although speeking Greek I think he was not well informed about the sexual practices among the Greek. The homosexul love between men and adolescents was the success of the Greek phalanx in battle; for if your lover besides you comes into mortal danger you release a strength and fury of which you have had no notion so far. And since the men found themselves so attractive it is no wonder that their women decided likewise among themselves.

B: When the Greeks felt the urge to practice sophisticated or extramarital sex they used the word „corinthizestai", to do like the Corinthians. The fame of this Paris of the old world certainly was known to Paul also. Small wonder, therefore, that he is especially lambasting them in his letters. The success rate is not known.

W: What is indigestable in my opinion is Paul's try to let marriage appear as the lesser evil only against free fornication. With that, he accorded prevention status to marriage, but not more.

That marriage could be arranged by caring parents or could end - also begin - in real love between two young people did not enter the mind of Paul the Single who was constantly torn between the production of his healthy glands and the totem of sin which he had erected against the human body.

B: In one place he is recommending his detached sexual status to all followers but is not specific at all just what this status is.

W: As I read it, he thought that he had effectively „killed“ his flesh from some point onward and was immune to sexual tentations for good -

B: Do you think that he emasculated himself?

W: Certainly not, otherwise he would have trumpeted this loudly. Whatever, this status must have come a long time after he wrote - to the Corinthians, of all people - that he reserved the same right for him as did all other apostles, also Peter and the brothers of Yeshua - to be accompanied constantly, and also probably on his travels, by a sister-wife, as he calls her, who apparently was looking after the bodily needs of the apostle, and I would not limit that to the food and laundry only.

B: Yes, I also have to smile a little bit whenever I read this. It makes the apostles a little bit more human and understanding as to the weakness of the flesh; all except Paul, because we read nowhere that he really exercised this prerogative.

W: So we see a torn Paul in any case, isn't it? Had he only tormented his brain and practised asceticism behind closed doors we would not mind. But he preached a mortal and sinful body which gives battle to the Spirit like an adversary of equal calibre, and this because the sheitan lurks in the body, having found an instrument which can deflect the human mind from the revelation. His verdict is simple: to hell with the body, and with sex also.

B: Could it be that he remembered sometimes that also he had a mother and a father?

W: I think that this little anomaly did not seriously reflect on his fanatic view.

B: Was pre- or extramarital sex the sin no. 1 for Paul?

W: Yes, mostly so. In some other line he stated that avarice is the mother of all sins. And yet in another place he argues that „the works of the flesh are manifest in adultery, fornication, uncleanness and lasciviousness" - so again the enemy no. 1.

B: I am still waiting for a few dissenting words on your part. Why are you not seeing yourself as Paul's attorney for a change? He is entitled to have a defense lawyer, no?

W: Why should I dream up some shyster arguments that could not exonerate him anyway? For instance that he had no concept of the primate parts of our human brain where the hypthalamus is still very much in control? That he was suffering from a neurosis which bordered on paranoia in matters of body, women and sex? That he was contradicting himself on these items not only once in his letters, probably depending on his mood and hardly ever on enlightenment from above? What do you want to hear?

B: Calm down, I did not mean earnestly that you would or could rush to his defense.

W: The defense rests, Your Honour.

B: We have picked around in details long enough and found them to be shabby, unfair, inconsistent and above all without any trace of love. This is my main accusation to Paul under this totem pole; in his dualism between the body, as the embodiment of all carnal creation, and the Spirit of the sum of God's love there was never a chance that the body needed or could receive divine love also.

He saw the body only as a constantly dangerous vehicle to which the Spirit was chained during terrestrial life. There were no grey zones in this black/white panel, no love and, what is more, no compassion with the body nor any joy to be derived from it which is natural and in unison with the creator of it.

W: I think that by his twisted attitude on the human body he prepared all such unholy developments in the young and adolescent church. Still in the young church there came the movement of the so-called holy men in Syria and Egypt who outdid each other in the castigation of body with self-inflicted tortures. It is only consequent that the eremites should experience their greatest temptations by apparitions of seductive women, as is reported and, not by the vision of sumptous meals or filled chalices. In fact Paul produced so many neurotics over the centuries that the guild of psychiatrists owes him a marble memorial, Paul and Freud hand in hand!

B: I cannot share your merriment, my friend. Since Paul rated matrimony down to a sexual pressure valve but praised virginity or non-marriage as a precious treasure that has to

(B): be locked away carefully it is he who invited uncounted thousands of men and women to enter the monasteries and convents where they could praise the Lord without too much hard work, regular if low-calory meals, evading taxes, subscription for military service and the unnerving marital ripostes on child education and household money.

In doing so these body-wary monks and nuns weakened the social system of their ethnic entities and undermined the economic growth and that of the population. Small wonder that the morals of these units got out of hand over the centuries and became the laughing-stock of the people, as e.g. the Carmina Burana have preserved it.

W: Again I have no defense material or witnesses who could effectively contest that this twisted thinking has pervaded the so-called christian church fully up to Lother who at least created some remedy for the body in the system. With the onset of the Counter-Reformation the body was called to order again, Paul's order.

The fundamental sects which were springing up, not to forget the humorless and unforgiving Puritans and Calvinists took Paul's gibes on the flesh more serious than Paul probably did.

The results were congregations of a high, yet twisted moral category but utterly devoid of a quality which Paul had destroyed once and for all: the joy of a healthy body, the joy of serving the Divine Spirit with body and consciousness, the relative low ranking of the sins of the flesh compared to cruelty, lack of compassion, denunciation, hate, lies, envy, vengeance. Still in our youth when there was talk of sin the priests rolled their eyes and pointed to Eve as the prime sinner. Silly people.

(W) To make it short: Paul has not only committed treason on the human being as such but far more so on the creative joy by which we can connect to the revelation through Yeshua. Instead of leading the believers by the hand over green and flowery meadows to the final goal he shooed them into swamps and on thorny trails telling them that there is no joy to be had on this earth and salvation can be had only by those who never smile.

Since he was twisted, barren and miserable he put this seal also on the faith.
I am quite positive that he fell out with his initial helpers and friends, who are mentioned in his letters, not so much over articles of faith but because of his intolerable, devastatingly negative state of mind.

B: And this is also why we fall out with him?

W: Also on this totem pole, certainly. We are not bowing before a devalued body, a besmirched sex nor before the chilly gust of unforgiving and inhuman coldness.

Original texts that have a bearing on Section 6:

Quotation	**Source**
.... for this cause God gave them up unto vile affectations: for even their women did change the natural use into that which is against nature. And likewise also the men, leaving the natural use of the women, burned in their lust one toward another	Rom I, 26-27
Therefore by the deeds of the law there shall no flesh be justified in his sight	id. III, 20
.... knowing this, that our old man is crucified with him, that the body of sin be destroyed that henceforth we should not serve sin	id. V, 6
For when we were in the flesh, the motions of sin, which were by the law, did work in our members to bring forth fruit unto death.	id. VII, 5
For we know that the law is spiritual: but I am carnal, sold under sin	id. VII, 14

Quotation	Source
For I know that in me, that is in my flesh, dwelleth no good thing	id. VII, 18
O wretched man that I am! Who shall deliver me from the body of this death? .... So then with the mind I myself serve the law of God; but with the flesh the law of sin	id. VII, 24
.... no condemnation (is) to them which are in Christ Jesus, who walk not after the flesh but after the Spirit.	id. VIII, 1
For what the law could not do, in that it was weak through the flesh, God sending his own Son in the likeness of sinful flesh	id. VIII, 3
For to be carnally minded is death; but to be spiritually minded is life and peace. Because the carnal mind is enmity against God	id. VIII, 6
So then they that are in the flesh cannot please God.	Rom, VIII, 8

Quotation	Source
Therefore, brethren, we are debtors, not to the flesh, to live after the flesh. For if you live after the flesh, you shall die; but if you through the Spirit do mortify the deeds of the body, you shall live.	id. VIII, 12
But put you on the Lord Jesus Christ, and make not provision for the flesh to fulfil the lusts thereof	id. XIII, 14
It is reported commonly that there is fornication among you, and such fornication as is not so much as named among the Gentiles	Cor I, V, 1
Now the body is not for fornication, but for the Lord	id. IV, 13
Know you no that your bodies are members of Christ?	id. VI, 15
Know you not that your body is the temple of the Holy Spirit which is in you ....?	id. VI, 19

Quotation	Source
It is good for a man not to touch a woman. Nevertheless, to avoid fornication, let every man have his own wife and let every woman have her own husband.	id. VII, 2
For I would that all men were even as I myself	id. VII, 7
.... he that gives (his virginal status) up in matrimony does well; but he who does not marry, does better	id. VII, 38
Have we not power to lead about a woman as a sister with us, as the other apostles do and the brethren of the Lord and Cephas? Should only Barnabas and I not have the authority to do likewise?	id. IX, 5
.... but I keep under my body and bring it into subjection: lest that by any means when I have preached to others, I myself should be dishonest.	id. IX, 27

Quotation	Source
And lest I should be exalted above measure through the abundance of the revelations, there was given to me a thorn in the flesh, the messenger of Satan, to beat me	Cor II, XII, 7
For, brethren, you have been called unto liberty, Only use not liberty for an occasion to the flesh, but by love serve one another.	Gal, V, 13
This I say then: walk in the Spirit and ye shall not fulfil the lust of flesh. For the flesh lusts against the Spirit, and the Spirit against the flesh, and these are contrary the one to the other	id. V, 16
Now the works of the flesh are manifest, which are these: adultery, fornication, uncleanness, lasciviousness	id. V, 19
And they that are Christ's have crucified the flesh with ist affections and lusts.	id. V, 24

Quotation	**Source**
Among whom also we all had our conversation in times past in the lusts of our flesh, fulfilling the desires of the flesh and of our thoughts	Eph I, 3
But the younger widows refuse: for when they have begun to wax wanton against Christ, they want to marry. They are damned because they have cast off their first faith. And withal they learn to be idle, wandering from house to house, and not only idle, but tattlers also and busybodies, speaking things which they ought not.	Tim. V, 11-13

7 The degradation of woman

W: We have tried to show in our previous book why the role of women in society suffered first from natural handicaps but, with time and „civilization“ progressing, much more so from man-made barriers, and if I say „man“ I mean THE MAN.

I think that with Paul we are not only having yet another skeptic of the female sex but the very source of the anti-female development in religion, law and social role of woman for the next 1.900 years, both in the so-called christian organizations and in Islam.

B: Are you not a little bit hasty in saying this? There is no question that Paul disliked women. But the role of women in the Hebrew religion, which was his arguing basis, had been cemented two milleniums before him already.

Judith and Esther were not the representatives of liberated Jewish women but single protagonists besides the silent army of child-rearing, milling, washing, cooking and copulating household utensils. So the depreciation of woman which appears in a dozen or more places in Paul's letters had been pre-ordained already long ago.

W: I am not going along with your thesis! What grew up since the stone age, what was adapted and codified in Hebrew law later, all this is a „natural“ process I should say, which occurred also in highly civilized China, where the development followed the same macho pattern.

(W): But Paul was the first who robbed women of their dignity in the name of the revelation through Yeshua. He wrote completely oblivious of Yeshuas's treatment of the women around him as equals under his message. Paul claims in so many instances that he received direct information from Yeshua on other subjects, e.g. on the - in our opinion - totally irrelevant issue of the Eucharist; why did he not receive supplementary information that he should not press women's faces in the mud?

B: Now this is certainly going too far! First of all, the revelation was not the message of liberation from traditional bondages - yes: alas, that is what we are saying 2.000 years afterwards, neither a call to free the slaves neither an exhortation to the male part of this planet to treat their wives as equal partners -

W: - and why not, please? Why was this Spirit from Yeshua sidestepping this screaming unjustness? The same Yeshua was served at invitations by slaves, something which he felt was quite in order apparently. Why did the Spirit not choose Spartacus instead? If already a human being is able to develop resentment and fury over treating human beings as animals, why could not a Divine Spirit confirm this and promulgate a new humanitarian order through his chosen instrument? An order that repaired the humiliation of woman also which had set in some 20.000 years ago? Can you tell me?

B: No, I cannot, because I feel like you. I have no explanation why the Spirit in Yeshua avoided these questions. The miserable explanation of the so-called christian organizations stinks, to say it bluntly. For them the casual outward serfdom of a male or female slave appeared irrelevant to the Spirit; what counted was the inner serfdom of all people, whether free or slave, towards sin.

(B): With such a cheap argument they managed to get by for almost 2.000 years, can you imagine that? In other words: human misery rates nothing against a human mind that is free of sin. Paul did not only condone this opinion but welded the chains of absolute subordination and of predestination on top of that. We shall discuss them in the next sections.

Coming back to your original question again: I also have no explanation, not even in the evolutionary view. To our issue we simply have to state that Paul found everything wonderfully prepared for him when he started from the social degradation of women into their spiritual defamation of character, because his lines are nothing less than that.

W: Let me take over here, please, because you are in a fury, no?

B: You can say that again. I am not courting the idea that it is a „holy“ furor, not for a second. It is a healthy furor combined with a downright reproach to the Spirit talking from Yeshua that he did not have the spiritual strength of a Spartacus in attacking these problems.

W: Perhaps we are too impatient again. Seen under an evolutionary period of roughly 2.000 years slavery has come to an end and women's lib is triumphantly on the march.

B: Certainly, and generation after generation suffered during these 2.000 years, was tortured, humiliated, killed because the revelation forgot them and Paul thought of them only in terms of souls to be saved, not of human beings.

W: I want to continue with the spiritual degradation of woman. Paul prepared the basis for a grateful Thomas Aquinas that women are not only feeble creatures in body, but also in mind, thanks to Eve of course. They must not participate in the discussions of men on holy matters, therefore, but listen demurely and silently. If any of them should really have the intelligence to inquire on some subject, then she should consult her husband at home afterwards. This inferred that husbands were always enlightened by their male and ruler status.

B: The call to submission came much more clearer, because he declared the man to be the head of the wife as Christ is the head of the church. The manifest hyperbole of this statement apparently did not trouble anybody - except perhaps women - over the centuries, neither clerics nor laymen. This clear dictum confirmed the second-class status of women not only within the house, but also in legislation and jurisdiction in the parts of the world where „Christianity“ reigned. Legislation on property owning and heritage rights was unabashedly tilted to favour the man, up to the hubris that the eldest male household member, even in dynasties, was the ruler of the woman, and if it was her bodily son.

W: Not only „christian“ countries were very satisfied with the macho basis they found fortified and enlarged by Paul. Mohammed and his semitic believers incorporated Paul's gender order gratefully into Islam. The Koran does not speak of Paul in this context but, as usual in these cases of adaptation, of the venerable prophet Isa/Yeshua. The role of woman in Islam was more tolerable than under „christian“ husbands, even if she had to share him with rival wives and, in later times, with a lot of concubines.

(W): Apparently Mohammed was of the opinion, in sharp contrast to Paul, that sexual intercourse gave wings to the mind of man instead of bogging it down in terrestrial mud. The property rights of the Moslem wife were far better than those of their „christian" sisters. The German Civil Code e.g. abolished the right of the husband to administrate the dowry only some 30 years ago. So much for women's lib!

B: We are being distracted by things beside the crucial points. Crucial in my opinion is the fact that Paul's arguments against women always bordered on saying that woman is evil, governed by the sheitan. Of course he was wise enough not to state this openly, so he confined himself to ruin their status up to our times as being a nuisance and seduction for the strong-willed and God-seeking man, biologically necessary, spiritually expendable. A second-class human being, nothing less.

W: Has anybody asked him what he thought of his mother? He might have been hard up for an answer.

B: In the orthodox Hebrew household in Tarsus he probably had a mother who answered to the traditional pattern fully. Certainly she never told him that she was suffering from the burden which religion had placed on her, and, who knows, she did not suffer at all?

W: It was also Paul who barred the way for women to be ordained priests in the „christian" churches. I had to smile when I read about the opening of the Anglican church in this matter, when there was a mass exodus of male priests who protested this unheard-of, un-biblical measure.

(W): You know that we are at odds in our opinion as to how priest churches will find their end, by chaos or civilized forms of transition. In my opinion the odds for civilized forms increase with the number of female clergy.

B: In Europe they are considering the introduction of altar girls besides altar boys as a major revolution already, very much against the warnings of the Polish Pope.

W: Speaking of him: do you think for a second that he would press for the veneration of Mary if it were found out that she was not a virgin? Never! Paul is twisting the brains of the so-called theologians still today.

B: All we have discussed here was justified and more or less substantial. The most substantial issue however, we have not yet covered: Paul has become guilty. Guilty in pushing aside one half of the population with the shyster argument that it is blocking the clear view of God. Guilty on the count of disdaining and violating human dignity of the same half. Guilty in prepairing and pre-condoning the witch hunts of later centuries. Guilty in preparing the ground for secular legislation that considered women to be of inferior legal status also. Guilty in bringing suppression, terror, persecution and suffering over women for 19 centuries who had no possibility to seek help, least of all from their „christian" churches or sects.

Of course he had no concept of evolution, we are not charging him with that. But having received supplementary enlightenings from above, as he is claiming, there was no enlightening on the fact apparently that woman ranges equally besides man, in body and spirit.

W: Do you know what I see before my eyes? There is a service going on in a church and the priest is turning to the congregation, book in hand and is saying „We are reading the epistle from St. Paul from ...“ and is staring then in disbelief as most of the female members rise and walk out of the church in silent protest. Do you think that we will witness this in our lifetime?

B: Possibly yes.

W: And what do we do?

B: Instead of axing another totem pole we see a statue lying in the mud, face down. When we clean her, we see the faces of millions of women before us. We are not going to put her on a pedestal; but we are uprighting her and giving her the place of honour that she deserves, before God and THE MAN. And we have pity on Paul.

Original texts having a bearing on Section 7

Quotation	Source
But I would have you know that the head of every man is Christ; and the head of the woman is the man.	Cor I, XI, 3
But every woman that prays or prophesies with her head uncovered dishonours her head: for that is even all one as if she were shaven. For if the woman be not covered let her also be shorn ...	id. XI, 5
For the man is not of the woman, but the woman of the man	id. XI, 9
Neither was the man created for the woman, but the woman for the man ...	id. XI, 9
Let your women keep silence in the community, for it is not permitted unto them to speak; but they are commanded to be under obedience, as also saith the law; and if they want to learn anything let them ask their husbands at home. For it is a shame for women to speak in the gathering. Or has the word of God come from you? Or came it unto you only?	id. XI, 34

Quotation	Source
The wives should submit themselves unto their husbands as unto the Lord. For the husband is the head of the wife, even as Christ is head of the church, and he is the saviour of its body. Therefore as the church is subject unto Christ, so let the wives be to their own husbands in all things.	Eph V, 22-24
.... let every one of you so love his wife even as himself; the wife however should go in fear of her husband.	id. V, 33
Wives, submit yourselves unto your husbands, as it is fit in the Lord.	Col III, 18
Let the woman learn in silence with all subjection. But I suffer not a woman to teach nor to govern her man, but to be silent. For Adam was formed first, then Eve. And Adam was not deceived but the woman was deceived in the transgression. However she shall be saved by giving birth to generations of children and if she stays in faith and charity and holiness in serenity.	Tim. I, II, 14-15

Quotation	Source
I will therefore that men pray everywhere, lifting up clean hands without wrath and doubting. In like manner also that women adorn themselves in modest apparel, with shamefacedness and sobriety; not with braided hair, or gold, or pearls, or costly array, but which becomes women professing piety by good works.	id. II, 9-10
But the younger widows refuse (from being elected) for when they have become wanton in Christ they want to marry. They are having damnation because they left their first faith. Besides they learn to be idle, wandering from house to house, not only idle but tattlers also and busybodies, speaking things which they ought not. I will therefore that the younger women marry, bear children, be mothers of their family, give no occasion to a detractor to speak ill of them. For some of them have turned to Satan already.	id. V, 11-5

Quotation	Source
It is good for a man not to touch a woman. Nevertheless, to avoid fornication, let every man have his own wife and let every woman have her own husband.	Cor I, VII, 1
He that is unmarried cares for the things which belong to the Lord, how he may please the Lord. But he that is married cares for the things that are of this world, how he may please his wife.	Cor I, VII, 32
Therefore he who gives away his virginity in marriage does well; he who does not marry, does better.	id. VII, 38

8 Predestination

B: If a religious group is granting extraordinary status to its true believers after bodily death, compared to all non-believers, then this arrogance is deplorable enough; seen this way the not-so-true followers and the non-believers are accorded lesser or minimal status - all of which is still corresponding to the intrinsic tangled logic of the spiritual leadership.

When, however, a church or sect is maintaining that its members are the only chosen people in the life to come, very exclusively so, that they have been pre-selected before their terrestrial birth already, and that other human beings are in the same manner excluded from the sunny side of the eternal order, then this is tantamount to a declaration of war against the rest of humanity -

W: - that is not the point, sorry to interrupt! The hyperbole turns into atrocity already before the combatants pass the threshold to eternity, here, in this world, in case the „chosen" people are striving for and are achieving political power, call it Jihad or Crusade. Because if they have arrived at power this is taken as the seal of their deity which is endorsing their superiority already here.

So it happened in the pre-christian world, notably so at the hands of the Israelites who shaped their „lebensraum" by extermination forays against other tribes; surely also in the Babylonian, Persian and Egyptain domains, only there it lacks the matter-of-fact documentation as we have it in the so-called Old Testament.

B: With the change of christianity from a persecuted, state-endangering movement to prescribed state religion, practically since the emperor Theodosius at the end of the 4th century, we are witnessing a new edition of an old text. The pre-selected believers become merciless, arrogant and joyous persecutors against the rest. Prostrate or die - there is no third choice.

W: Humanity and evolution are hiding their face in sorrow. But we have to realize that these developments are only the tip of the iceberg. A special adjective still has to be found for those criminal organizations - I am choosing the wording with all deliberation - which add the ultimate insult or irony of their crippled faith: that other human beings may strive to the best of their efforts to live according to the expectations of the organization's belief, but it will not do them any good because they are not listed in the book of salvation above. No piety, no good deeds will make them eligible. Sorry, the boat is full.

B: May I propose the adjective? Very plainly: Meschugge, not that this is giving them any excuse.

W: I wonder if you are having another one in store for the next category, which we are also meeting right and left on our planet: It is another step further into conceit and mercilessness. What I have said before is, in the so-called christian context, already the sin against the Spirit, because the outcasts are maintaining with due right that God is evil; they are barred entry, full stop.

Now, if the „true" believers would draw the line here and would grant them the permanent exitus status, i.e. that after bodily death these hapless creatures are non-existant any more, extinguished forever, even this morsel of pity would have to be

(W): recognized in their favour. But no, they maintain, because these men/women were living outside the grace of God, which was so ordained for them from the beginning of this cosmos, they will have to suffer in eternity; perhaps not so much as downright evildoers, but eternal spiritual pain nevertheless. Are you having now the fitting adjective for the triumphantly chosen?

B: Yes. Paranoids.

W: I think that it is high time now to analyze how Paul's teachings fit into these revolting scenarios. No. 1, erecting the rule of the chosen people in terrestrial times?

B: No, there is no call to arms in his writings. On the contrary he is advising great care not to disturb the ordained powers, regardless of their secular claims.

W: Granted. For what happened later in this respect he was welcome ammunition but he did not pull the trigger. A wedding of so-called christian faith and absolute secular power was beyond the horizon of his expectations. If he had held it possible at his time he would have sounded all carillons of triumph.
And now, No. 2: the choice by God's grace, where striving or good deeds are simply neglected?

B: Yes, that is Paul's legacy, alas. The quotations at the end of this section document this in glaring detail and with no possibility of rationalization or excuse.

W: Finally, scenario No. 3: the unlucky humans shall also suffer eternally?

B: There we have Paul the blind fanatic raging again. Yes, he is guilty of this most unfair concept which the human mind can ever produce: eternal bliss for the pre-selected, eternal pain for the non-selected. Shrugging his shoulders, not even a word of compassion, finis.

W: Can Paul be exonerated on the grounds that the same elitist claim had been propagated by the Hebrew belief? That he simply usurped it for the belief in his Christ?

B: If we agree that not a shimmer of a Holy Spirit worked in him, we may put it sadly ad acta, to be forgotten as soon as possible. Under his thinly veiled claim that he did so, however, we are telling him: Either you lie, Paul, or I do not want to be part of this development, because this is not the God of the revelation through Yeshua but the Jahve deity of your ancestors. If this deity is also governing eternity, please have me extinguished in this very moment, not remembering, not being remembered, non-existant. And to hell with your deity!

W: It is the historical merit of Luther that he also told Paul squarely: not so! The intentions and deeds in this bodily life determine our transmortal existence. It is deplorable on the other hand that Luther rebelled to this venom only and, not to forget, also to the highly unnecessary question of the nature of the Eucharist -

B: Objection! Unnecessary and unimportant for us, but not for the discussions of his time. The „esti" - it is, not only seemingly, which Huldrich Zwingli wrote on the tablecloth between them in the famous Marburg dispute, was not an academic question but carried the danger of life in it.

W: All right, let it be. Luther also declared the direct responsibility of man/woman before God, without mediators. So far, so good, this had been one of the tenets of Islam seven hundred years before him. And why did the Lutherans employ priests then, please? The confessional was abolished, of course, cutting a major breach into the despondency of laymen, laywomen, princes and kings from Rome-loyal priests.

B: We are getting distracted, my friend. Let's reserve this for another book, maybe.

W: Sorry, you are right. I think we should try to see instead whether this extreme mercilessness of predestination has pervaded younger history or our times. In our terminology it is nothing less than the abolition of free will -

B: If it were only that! If the pre-selected saints would say that there is no free will, we would file this in the drawer of thoughtless intransigence and intolerance. But they are pushing to the end of the spectrum by saying that the poor beings had free will, of course; but God knew beforehand how they would use this free will, turning to his revelation, neglecting it or turning actively against it. This is the ultimate perversion of evolution.

W: Sorry to contradict you! This is not yet the ultimate perversion. A mental depravity that cannot be surpassed in my opinion is the belief that the chosen few can be identified in this terrestrial life already, not only in the moment of reckoning. Because, as Paul has been telling them, it can be seen already on this earth how all things work out beautifully for those how are adhering to the right faith, meaning that success in economic affairs and politics is already the red carpet here on which the chosen proceed to eternal bliss.

B: Do you mean to say that, in reverse: bad luck, lack of education, poverty, illness, even being naive and trusting is the mark of the non-chosen?

W: You just have to ask Calvin. He was exactly of that opinion and formed his creed of the successful chosen that makes the shivers run over your back still today.

B: But Calvinism is a widespread faith still today. Do they all still adhere to this elitist mercilessness?

W: If you ask a member of their faith, the answer is that this aspect is not a credo of their belief any more, but can be seen allegorically -

B: By that they are reducing their faith practically to a sort of a Higher Rotary Club, no?

W: As long as they are adhering to their exclusive calling, yes.
The Divine Spirit is not in them, let alone evolution.

B: Just to put „the fear of God“ into you, I am giving you a statement of the Dutch Rigorists, who wrote a riposte to their detractors, clarifying their predestined status. The year is 1610:

> „After Adam's fall God had exempted a certain number of people from damnation and ... ordained them for salvation through Christ ... In this choice of grace God does not consider the faith or conversion but acts only according to his judgement.
> God has sent his son, Christ, to redeem the chosen ones, and only them:“

W: Hearing this I feel icy fingertips going down my spine. Imagine that these men were loving fathers and husbands! How is it possible that they stripped love and pity when leaving their doorstep?

B: Because Paul told them so, and if not, he was their mental basis. His and their deity had a clear cry of battle: no prisoners!

W: I get physically sick, sorry, I cannot continue this discussion any more.

B: We need no more proof of Paul's guilt. He is in up to his neck, Spirit or no Spirit, it does not natter in the last consequence.

W: And what are we doing to this totem pole of his?

B: In view of the enormity of the issue, we are not simply axing it down. We are burning it with the flames of humanity, compassion and evolution in a giant inferno that finishes forever any notion of predestination of populations, creeds or individuals. It shines on the past generations who have suffered to an extent we cannot imagine; it shines on the path of evolution which is able to smile on this period of aberration, contrary to us.

W: And what about Paul?

B: Hide your head, Paul!

Original texts having a bearing on Section 8:

Quotation	Source
To all that are in Rome, beloved of God, called to be saints	Rom I, 7
For as many have sinned without law shall also perish without law; and as many as have sinned in the law shall be judged by the law	Rom II, 12
And we know that all things work together for good to them that love God, those who are called by his plan. For those whom he did foreknow he did predestinate them to become conformed to the image of his Son so that he might be the firstborn among many brethren. Moreover, whom he did predestinate he has also called; and whom he has called, them he had also justified; and whom he justified, them he also glorified.	Rom VIII, 28-30

Quotation	Source
For he says to Moses: „I have mercy on whom I have mercy and I have compassion on whom I have compassion.“ Therefore it's not up to those who are willing and giving effort but only up to the mercy of God ... so he is showing mercy to whom he wants and hardens whom he wants to ... Oh man, who are you that you want to argue with God? Shall a formed thing speak to him who formed it: Why have you made me so? Has not the potter power over the clay, to make from the same lump a vessel that merits honour and another that is a shame? .... he endured with long patience the vessels of wrath fit for destruction; and that he might make known the riches of his glory on the vessels of mercy which he had prepared for glory beforehand.	Rom IX, 15-23
.... so then at this present time also there is a remnant according to the choice of grace. And if by grace, it does not come from works, otherwise grace would not be grace.	Rom XI, 5

Quotation	Source
.... to them called to be saints	Cor I, I, 2
But unto them who are called, both Jews and Greeks (we preach Christ the crucified)	Cor I, I, 24
But when it pleased God who singled me out since being in my mother's womb and called me by his grace	Gal I, 15
According as he has chosen us in him before the creation of the world ...	Eph I, 4
For by grace you are saved, through faith and not of yourselves, this is the gift of God.	Eph II, 8
For it is God who works in you the will and the deed according to his good will	Phil II, 13
.... by grace you are saved	Eph II, 5

Quotation	**Source**
This is why God is sending them strong delusions that they should believe in lie; and that all should be judged who believe not in the truth but consented to injustice.	Thess II, 11-12
Because you have come ... to congregation of the first ones which are written down in heaven	Heb XII, 23
But if our gospel be hid, it is hid to them that are lost. In whom the god of this world has blinded the minds of them who believe not, so that the light of the glory of Christ, who is the image of God, should not shine on them	Cor II, IV, 4

9 Slaves and Masters

W: When we decided to write this book we shook hands on our intention not be the umpteenth academic commentary on Paul but to use clear and simple language, isn`t it?

B: So be it. But why are you bringing this up?

W: Because especially this section needs a conditioning of the reader, male or female, before we come back to the more detached view of a historian or philosopher. In other words: we must get under the skin of our reader first!

B: I doubt whether your approach is very helpful. We decided to use plain language and have kept our promise so far, I think. Why do you see the necessity to use dramatic language in this section? Because that is what you are up to, no?

W: Yes, very much so. The reason is that in my opinion Paul is probably going to receive the full benefit of the „historical context" and that we have to search a little deeper - or higher - for what is at the roots of his teachings in this respect. In order to show now the full brutality and mercilessness of the thinking I want to draw a background canvas first. Agreed?

B: Half-heartedly so. I doubt whether this will bring us a plus of evolutionary insight, but have your way!

W: Transform yourself back for 1.000 years. You are living in a city which is heavily fortified by walls, towers and war machinery. Your rulers are, let us say, tolerable. You are a loyal citizen, trained in warfare. You are also a family father, having a loving wife and at least eight children ranging from 18 down to years.

Your bliss is ruined because an army of intruders, of whatever origin, is demanding the surrender of your city. The conditions are clear and cruel: if the city opens her gates without resistance there will be only looting, with a few occasional rapes. If, however, the city refuses, all inhabitants are forfeited, in clearer terms: all throats will be cut, of men, women, old, young, and of babies.

Holding the enemy in contempt, the city elders refuse the offer. They decide to fight the enemy. But for whatever reasons, be it lack of nourishment, water, sheer treason, military superiority or by utter negligence - as with Byzantium in 1453 - the enemy penetrates into your city. Your defence forces, poorly coordinated, are routed almost instantly.

The stone age wrath of the invaders calls for blood - of every living being in your city, yours, that of your wife, that of your children, and you, being very much alone now after the din of battle and after your friends have been slain, you have no more power to offer a trade for anything. You, your beloved wife and your beloved children are doomed. The next enemy soldier will slit the throats of you all.

But he doesn't. Instead he is first raping your wife with a knife held by his comrades to your throat, and you are not moving an inch. And then they are tying the hands behind,

(W): yours first, then your wife's, then of your children who are usable as slaves, and then they march you off to the slave trader who has accompanied the victor's forces from the beginning of the invasion. He is looking at you, your wife and your children as if they were cattle. Your master, the enemy soldier who is bringing you for sale, will be content to receive the minimum price. He and his comrades are eager to forage into the city again to bring more flesh.

This was the last time you saw your wife and children, with heart-rendering cries of despair by you and them. And then you were carted off into slavery. Sold in whatever slave market offered the best prices, down to the later slave market in Venice which still is bearing the ignominious name of „Riva degli schiavoni", landing shore of slaves.

B: I think that you covered the starting issue quite markedly. This saves me to add the misery of all the African slaves who were also caught like cattle and were transported under indescribable conditions to the so-called New World.

W: I am glad that you tolerated my long introduction.

B: Certainly. But there is one fundamental issue in slavery, as you very lucidly described it in your historic example: slavery in these times, and we are speaking of the times of Paul, was held to be the grace of him who could kill this person by his unquestioned right of war. But he did not exercise this right. He saw more profit in selling this person into slavery; in any battle there were the slave traders following the troops with thousands of clamps and chains.

W: I think that we have cleared the scenery enough now to talk about Paul's notions on slaves and masters, no?

B: Let's get started!

W: First of all, as we said already, we have to give Paul the man the benefit of the historical context. Serfdom and slavery was for him an undisputable fact also in the Hebrew system. He neither saw a legal nor a social necessity to change this aspect. And it looked very humanitarian to him and all others, because life was preserved instead of extinguished by the victor.

B: But deeply inside he must have felt that something was severely wrong in degrading human beings to the status of cattle. Why would he have admonished the slaves among his followers to serve their masters without any reservations, even with joy? And not to become uppity and demanding their freedom when their masters also embraced Paul's teachings?

W: This is easy to explain. He considered the masters of slaves to be the same ordained power over people as elected leaders or dictators. They had to be obeyed because this pleased his God, even if the masters were unjust or sadistic. From Paul there was no consolation.

B: Was there any redress for tormented slaves at all in these times?

W: Hardly. There existed a municipal authority in Rome which, in cases of extreme cruelty to slaves, could forbid certain male or female masters to hold slaves; more or less in the same way as if a present-day court would rule that somebody would not be allowed to own animals any more.

(W): Generally, however, a slave was never allowed to raise accusations against his/her master. Any slave who violated this rule faced certain death, by the court, mind you, not by his master who had the right to kill him or her at any given time. The only exception where an accusation of the master went unpunished was in cases of high treason.

To top it all, the law called for the excution of all slaves in a household where the master was murdered by a slave or unknown person. We have the story of such a happening on record in Rome, where all 400 slaves of a murdered patron were executed without mercy. The sheer monstrosity of this action compelled the population to plead for their lives with the Senate, to no avail. The argument was that by creating such a precedent no master could sleep quietly any more in the future.

B: And the circus games and the mines needed constant supply, not to forget: ad bestias, ad minas!

W: The whole backward view is of such incredible atrocity that it makes you sick, and not only since Mrs. Harriet Beecher Stowe.

To come back to our inquiry: is Paul to be accused of having promoted slavery so that this perverse instrument could survive all so-called christian centuries until the 19th one? And mind you, it was not the so-called christian churches or a pope who brought about the change, but the humanitarian movements which started in Britain in the 18th century. It took another hundred years to have it accomplished. But we have clandestine pockets of slavery still today, e.g. in the Sudan or in India.

B: To answer your question: we must acquit Paul on the accusation of having promoted slavery.

W: But what about the fact that he condoned it?

B: As we have said already Paul the man cannot be held responsible for his attitude since it corresponded to the legal and social context of his time.

W: So the Holy Spirit in him condoned this monstrosity also?

B: Ah, here we are coming now to the deeper roots! For once, I doubt very much that Paul wrote under the influence of a Divine Spirit, nor here nor elsewhere. We have to look for some other authority, therefore, before and above him that made him stay in the accepted codex of his time.

W: You can be referring only to Yeshua, no?

B: To the Spirit talking intermittently from Yeshua, in order to be precise. We made this vital distinction in our „Stone Age Of Faith“ already and do not have to enter into the issue all over again here, therefore. Yes, I mean this Spirit. Yeshua was never prompted to speak out against the instrument of slavery; there is no mentioning of it in all four reports.

Now, there are only two possible avenues of explanation: for one, the Spirit did not consider slavery to be a hindrance to approach the revelation, because all men are alike

(B): before God. The fact that slaves are kept in bondage or misery for the short span of their earthly life does not count very much or brings them additional merit.

The second explanation is that the same Spirit talking from Yeshua saw in slavery another proof for the depravity and arrogance of our species which he „heartily" detested, if this word is allowed, and said so several times. This Spirit saw the deficit in human consciousness very well; but it also saw the path of evolution, past and future, and saw in this also the terrestrial year of 1865, and that of 1998 which still does not know a written Charta Of Human Rights, to be applied also forcibly on nations, if need be.

W: If you are voicing these possibilities you are inferring that the evolution in other habitats avoids the preparedness to enslave its own kind, in the minds of the thinking creatures there?

B: I consider this to be a strong probability, yes, because serfdom or slavery is absolutely anti-evolutionary.

W: It is also against the essence of the revelation through Yeshua, of the same Yeshua who was waited upon by slaves when having dinners with the rich - and never spoke out against it.

B: Are you still holding it against him?

W: I take the liberty of my free will to hold it against the Spirit which was talking through him against many other deficits of the human race, but never against this scarlet-red injustice.

Why was this Spirit not with Spartacus? If the monstrosity of slavery could move an able man like Spartacus, why should it not move a Divine Spirit? Or could it be that this Spirit from Yeshua was not fully competent here also, as we have seen in other instances?

B: We shall not have the answer to that in this life. But looking back on the 6.000 crosses on which the Romans nailed the defeated rest of Spartacus'brave army I also feel that something went terribly wrong with the human mind long before him and that something vital is missing in the revelation through Yeshua.

W: What is our final word on Paul now in this respect?

B: No Holy Spirit and not guilty.

Original texts having a bearing on Section 9:

Quotation	**Source**
Exhort the slaves to be obedient unto their own masters and to please them well in all things. No back talk; no cheating, but show good will in all things, so that they adorn the teaching of our God-Saviour in all things.	Titum II, 9-10
You have been called to serfdom? Care not for it! But if you should be freed, use it rather! For he who is called a slave in the Lord, he is a freeman of the Lord. Likewise also the free man who is called is a slave of the Christ. You are bought with a price, but be you not the slaves of men. Everybody who is called, brethren, he should stay in this state before God.	Cor I, VII, 21-24
You slaves, obey your bodily masters in fear and anguish, in the natural simplicity of your hearts, same as to the Christ. Not with eye service to please men, but as the slaves of the Christ, doing the will of God from your mind with good will, as if you	Eph VI, 5-9

Quotation	Source
were serving the Lord and not the men, knowing that if anybody does something good, this is retributed to him by the Lord, be he a slave or a free man. And you, masters, do the same unto them, not using threats and keeping in mind that their and your Lord is in heaven and that there is no status of the person before him.	
You slaves, obey in all things to your bodily masters. Not with eye-service, in order to please men, but in the simplicity of your heart and in the fear of God. And whatever you are doing, do it from your mind as if you were doing it for the Lord and not for men, knowing that from the Lord you will accept your reward of inheritance. For you are the slaves of Christ the Lord. But he who does wrong will receive back the wrong he has done, without status of person before God. You masters, give to your slaves what is just and fair and remember that you are having a master in heaven.	Col III, 22-25 Col IV, 1

Quotation	Source
The serfs who are under the yoke of slavery should treat their masters with all due honour so that the name of the Lord and (our) teaching may not be blasphemed. Those who are having believing masters should not rate them less because they are brethren, but they should do more service to them because they also are believers and beloved, partaking in the blessing. Teach and underline this!	Tim I. VI, 1-2
You slaves, be subject to your masters with all due fear. Not only to the good and gentle ones, but also to the wayward ones. Because this is the grace if someone suffers in thinking of God his unjust treatment. For what glory is there in suffering beatings for things you have done badly? But if you suffer for things having done rightly you shall merit grace with God. ... For this you are called, because Christ also suffered for us, leaving us the example that we should follow his steps	Peter I, II, 18-23

10 The ordained powers

B: When we hear the admonishments of Paul - and likewise those of Peter - to their converts that they should accept their worldly rulers not with clenched teeth but as their wardens who have invariably been installed by God we are having some important questions to ask in retrospect, correct?

W: Correct so far only. You already sailed around one of the cliffs by saying „when looking back“; with that you have admitted implicitly that the general view of Paul's time plays the major role in this issue and not Paul - or Peter for that - himself, but that they were echoing the general belief of their times, be it Hebrew, Greek, or Roman -

B: Objection! Objection several times, my friend! If you are referring to the dubious „historical context“ of which we talked in the beginning of this book, then you are forgetting apparently that the Greek had already a long and bloody history of toppling governments or autocrats long before the birth of Yeshua. So it was with the Romans; may I remind you only that Cesar crossed the Rubicon in 49 B.C.?

W: I am not contesting these facts. You only were a little bit hasty and did not let me finish. Perhaps I should have said that Paul - let's stay only with him from now on - echoed the general yearn of their times, be it Hebrew, Greek, or Roman. A Hebrew yearn it was also because Israel knew very well to what sort of tetrarchs it was exposed to at these times.

B: The texts of Paul are not insinuating anywhere that the population of any country should close their eyes before the arbitrary, biased or downright criminal rule of their leaders. On the contrary they say that any terrestrial power that is can exist only because it has been installed by God. Full stop.

W: What you want to say is that secular power, no matter how their leading characters came into it, was a blank cheque by God into which they could fill in the amount and the beneficiary at their discretion?

B: If you subscribe to Paul, yes. For him only one thing counted: peace with the secular power. He apparently was forgetting the example that Peter and Yochanaan had set when they told their superiors that God must be obeyed more than man. In his letters there is no reference to the flagellation these two had to suffer because they pushed this credo home into the faces of the Sanhedrin.

W: But where is any reservation of this sort in Peter's letters later on? None, just as none is in Paul's writings. I am quite sure, however, that Peter, upon learning of the unconditional surrender of Paul to the secular powers - because it is nothing else - had protested. But if so, we are having no report on it.

B: Unconditional surrender? And what was Paul dying for finally, please?

W: Brace yourself, my friend: he was dying for a misunderstanding to which Pilate already was a victim because of insufficient grant - or in case of Yeshua - will of having due hearing. In both cases there were probably the same catchwords: not king of this world,

(W): but supreme king of the universe. The catchword „king“, however, was the trigger in both cases: high treason, because the emperor is the sole ruler of this world and his genius - let us translate it as „soul“, is God-like after bodily death. So: any king who is not paying tribute to him is a rebel, or worse, a contender for the imperial throne.

B: If you read the four reports on Yeshua you can see how the Sanhedrin fed exactly this line of reasoning - very much against their intrinsic belief - to Pilate. Corrupt as he was, this was the acid test of his loyalty. The death verdict against Yeshua was a clear - though reluctant - pledge of allegiance to the emperor. He could not risk having the Hebrews to complain in Rome against his attitude. So went Yeshua.

W: And so went Paul?

B: Hardly. Having the Roman citizenship, and putting claim to it, he faced the emperor, Nero probably. But then, knowing Paul's temperament from his letters, and because he also prepared very long for this moment, fervently hoping that in converting the emperor to the revelation of Yeshua - or how he saw it - we can safely assume that he fell by sheer exitement into the style of his letters.

W: And the emperor turned down his thumb?

B: Probably there was not even a written accusation. We do not know. But when Paul opened up the rhetoric as reported in the Acts or in his letters, it is safe to assume that the emperor considered his convictions not as a threat to his throne but simply as a boring and loud nuisance of which he wanted to get rid of urgently: thumb down.

W: It would be interesting to know what Paul felt in this moment about the ordained powers of the world? Still God - installed?

B: If not sooner, that was the moment when it was clear to Paul that the ordained powers of the world are not installed by God but that they are wily, corrupt, arbitrary, cruel and have above all a one-track intention: to stay in power and to extend it.

W: Would he have re-written the corresponding texts in his letters if he had a chance to do so?

B: I am sure he would have not done it. First of all because he would have to admit having committed a grave error, which certainly was not his forte. Secondly he would have had to offer a credible substitute, but which? Check out your wordly governments whether they correspond at least to a humanitarian minimum? This concept, as we know looking backward, was not anchored in the common consciousness of these times. But feeling oppressed and exploited, which needs no markers of consciousness because of its manifest misery, tears and blood, should they consider revolution?

W: The historical rhetoric on this issue can be boiled down very simply to the question: who was faster? Was it the ground wave of human insight, 1800 years before Rousseau, that man is born free but is still languishing in irons, or was it Paul's uncritical dictum that the powers of this world are not only God-tolerated, with all their warts, but clearly and unmistakably God-wanted?

B: History has given the answer: Paul was faster. The young so-called christian church would not have succeeded if Constantine had not given his state tolerance and his successor Theodosius had not succumbed to the demands of ever eager, ever merciless leaders of new spiritual movements to declare the so-called christian faith to be the proscribed state religion.

If it was not Constantine, who practically ruled the decisions of the Council of Nikea, then it was Theodosius who recognized again the utterly beautiful, logical and inescapable order of having a God-installed secular system - for which he probably had a pagan shrug only - but at the same time a state religion that was the guardian not only of her truths but also of the supporting terrestrial administration. A tandem system - unbeatable.

W: And you claim that here is Paul's fatal mistake, isn't it?

B: We are coming back to the beginning of our discussion. What we read in Paul's letters is the exhortation to the believers to accept worldy power not only as a God-tolerated but as a God-wanted system, without any hints of relativity as to how this present „ordained" power came into existence, be it by tradition, vote, coup d'etat, revolution or whatever. Therefore we have to ask Paul: have you never read history before you, Hebrew, Greek or Roman?
How can you dare to present this simplistic view to your converts?
In short: what are you teaching them for the present and the future, Paul?

W: In answering that we have two options. We can take the super-flying view or the timid one.

The super-flying view reads as following, assumed original tone of Paul: „We all know that the ordained powers of this world have come into power mostly by questionable means. Let this not disturb you, followers of Christ. Because lastly, it is irrelevant to us. The essential thing which we expect of the rulers is that they leave us in peace to practice our religion according to revelation and tradition. If they do so, we are not having a problem with them and, to accentuate this very clearly, we are loyal citizens. We pay taxes, follow a call to arms and support the state in every other respect.“

Now, would you take the option of timidity?

B: I try to, quoting an imaginary Paul again:

„Brethren, do not get into trouble with the secular power that is ruling you. Not because you are recognizing that man's basic values are trodden down by them every day and that you are not having the power to stay that. No. These powers are a trial on our belief which we have to overcome. Perhaps not in our generation, but certainly so in the future ones. And, please, be careful about the kingdom of Christ. Whenever you say that our Christ is a king you are challenging the terrestrial claims of the existing powers to which they will react swiftly and mercilessly. On the other hand, they will leave you not enough time to explain nor do they understand that this kingdom is certainly not of this world. In short, they will accuse you of high treason; you will die. So: be careful, be clever, be silent.“

W: Objection in full! This never was the intention of Paul. He told them to raise their voice wether there was an appropriate occasion or not. He never told them to put incense on the coals before the emperor's statue just to placate the state belief of his genius. He told them to be defenders of the revelation of Yeshua. Or do you read anything else in his letters?

B: Now don't jump at me if I say that I do not know.
Firstly, I doubt very much that Paul was able to transport the essentials of Yeshua's revelation to his converts. My main argument is that the heavy cargo of his Hebrew tradition was saddled by him on the message conveyed by the Spirit through Yeshua, practically as a sort of filter. Out of this message came only the elements which were sensibly connecting to Hebrew tradition, the so-called Old Testament. Do not ask me about his enlightenement in the Holy Spirit. We reserve this for the end of this book.

Secondly, I feel that Paul was very much aware that the message through Yeshua was a revolutionary message, regardless of the fact that it was addressed to masters and slaves alike without any difference. He was also very acutely aware that the teachings of his Christ meant an upheaval of values applied so far to the veneration of a God and to the treatment of human beings.

Recognizing the dynamite potential of the revelation through Yeshua, Paul was weighing the survival potential of the new faith and found that it would not survive if it went into a frontal assault against the terrestrial powers, at least not if the believers were an outcast minority.

W: But, writing in the Holy Spirit that he thought he had, could he not foresee the silver lining on the horizon, nor the triumph of the state religion?

B: I do not want to comment on that here.

W: I am asking you directly: has Paul become guilty in preaching the unquestioning obeisance to the secular power, whatever its nature?

B: Yes, undoubtedly he is guilty, and we are not going any further in our analysis as we have done already. He clearly is the architect of the unholy marriage of state and church that brought misery on humanity since practically the year of 385 A.C., when an empereror Theodosius declared the Christian belief to be the state religion - with the ensuing barbaric persecutions of the pagan believers. But since it is always the victor who writes history, we have few witness reports on this.

W: I am sorry, but I am pushing Paul's guilt much further.
Considering all historical excuses that he had no notion at his time of democracies, inspite of the Greek models, or of republics, inspite of the Roman history, one thing should have stood out in his mind over all other matters, as parallels to Hebrew history, that especially feudal systems were based on blank ruthlessness, connivance, murder and genocide. Paul was an intelligent man with a profound education, if it were only in the Hebrew history -

B: - and there is the crux of his thinking, sorry to interrupt! Had he been brought up in the Greek or Roman history, he would have learned to differentiate. But in the Hebrew faith any social or political development was tied to a higher order - God's orders.

(B): An order of their deity was also the occupation of Israel by the Romans - a penalty for non-compliance with contractual agreements, on his part.
Putting the tenet of God-ordained secular powers high above anything else therefore, Paul saw in the errors, cruelties, mercilessness of systems only timely aberrations that would quickly be healed by time.

W: What surprises us is that he knew the Babylonian captivity and other nadir points of his national history and was still maintaining that the powers which brought them on were God-ordained ones?

B: I doubt that he thought of them in the moment when he was dictating his letters.

W: I have a question of utmost importance now: can we hold Paul at least co-responsible for the atrocities that secular powers committed on humans, be it by the bidding of churches or on their own?

B: Yes, Paul is guilty. Not as the protagonist of an inquisition, Hitler, Stalin, Alba or Pol Pot. But he stifled resistance in the so-called christian churches or sects against inhuman practices because he rendered to the ordained powers his unmitigated argument of obeisance. They used it for all their cruelties and stifled their allied churches or sects with his literal rulings.

W: Do you think that this is also the ultimate reason why a Pope Pius XII dared not to speak out clearly against the Shoa?

B: No, I think that he had all the right intentions but dared not to speak out to foment the rebellion of catholic believers in the Nazi domain; instead he trusted his personal ties as a former Nuntius to Hitler - and failed. He learned to late that when it comes to crucial issues diplomacy is but a blunt weapon.

W: How many divisions does the Pope have?

B: I expected that famous riposte of Stalin to Molotov. Had the Pope really activated his divisions by telling them through his church - at the danger of life for the priests reading this from the pulpit of course - he would have warned about 10 millions of them in Germany and occupied Austria. This was, in terms of military potential, more than half of the German army.

W: But he did not risk it, as we know?

B: No, alas. Some credible writers accord it to the fact that his enemy no. 1 was socialism, Soviet style. As long as Hitler was battling it, he was clearly the minor evil, Shoa or not.

W: In defense of Paul we have to say that it was impossible for him to foresee all the unsavoury intertwining of church or sect organizations with the powers of this world.

Moreover we have to consider that these organizations, somewhere along their track, lost their set of values. The preservation of the organization became the primary goal. For this, they suppressed also tenets of their belief, just to remain the trusted partners of the secular powers.

B: If we want to pass a final comment on Paul's teachings on the ordained powers of this world, what would we say?

W: First of all, that he was unable apparently to imagine that a secular power had come into power without the help of God and to stay in this power, no matter how it treats their subjects.
Secondly when reading Paul we only see wordly governments who are corresponding to the rare species of philosopher-kings like Ashoka, the Hohenstaufen Frederic II, Salah-Ed-Din or Frederic II of Prussia. Most governments of the ancient western world were not so, but were mixtures of bigotry, intolerance, cruelty and spiritual oppression. Was Paul really under the impression that worldly governments are God-sent and are doing invariably what is best for their subjects?

B: Let us give him the benefit of doubt, which means that he was not well enough educated and, above all, was not much of a critical mind when it came to realpolitik. If we grant him an exit out of this dilemma we should say that he was aware of all these historical, political and social components but rated them nil against the existence of the message coming through Yeshua.

W: And there I disagree for the last time in this section, but very earnestly so! If Paul, in enlightened status or simply remembering Jewish, Greek or Roman history had understood the „christian" values of a citizen correctly, he would have demanded or emphasized to his converts to see the political powers under a humanitarian pattern in the first line. Any power that is not respecting this basic tenet should not receive political power from its subjects, right?

B: My dear friend, are you not realizing that you are hopelessly caught in democratic notions? When 2.000 years ago somebody came to power it was by murdering his father and brothers. And when on his throne, he was the „ordained power" as Paul is writing. It does not matter at all on what legal or illegal mechanism a ruler came into power. When he was, he was. Again, for Paul he was the ordained power.

W: So what are we putting at the end of this section?

B: Paul paved the road to suppression and exploitation of people who believed him that their suppressors were God-sent and had to be obeyed. According to him they should even close their eyes to the cruelties inflicted by the secular power unto those who rebelled against certain tenets of commanded belief - it was the God-sent revenger and secular arm of the one and only faith - he did not foresee these atrocities of course, but he was the later common claim of both, clergy and state.

W: Again, a final comment please!

B: May God have mercy on you for this, Paul!

Original texts that have a bearing on Section 10:

Quotation	**Source**
Let every soul be subject unto the higher powers. For there is no power but of God: The powers that be are ordained by God. Whosoever resists the power, resists the ordinance of God; and they that resist shall receive to themselves damnation. For rulers are not a terror to good works, but to the evil. Are you not fearing the power? Do that which is good and you shall have praise of the same. For he is the minister of God to thee for good. But if you do which is evil, be afraid! For he bears the sword not in vain; for he is the minister of God, the revenger in the wrath to the evildoer. Therefore you must subject yourself, not only because of the wrath, but also because of your own conscience. Therefore pay also tribute because they are God's ministers and serve him in doing so.	Rom XIII, 1-6

Quotation	Sources
I exhort therefore that first of all supplications, prayers, intercessions and thanksgiving be made for all men; For kings, and for all that are in authority, that we may lead a quiet and peaceful life in all piety and chastity ...	Timoth I, II, 2
Admonish them to be subject to the rulers and powers, to obey their orders	Titum, III, 1

For comparison:

Fear God. Honour the king.	Peter I, II, 17
Submit yourself to every ordinance of man for the Lord's sake, whether it be to the king as the supreme, or unto governors that are sent by him for the punishment of evildoers and for the praise of the good ones	Peter I, II, 13-15

11 Vengeance and curses

B: We have come to realize that Paul preached and wrote very often in a state of excitement that made it hard for him to marshal his thoughts. His listeners and readers may have wondered if there was some obsession in him; since they were afraid of him on these occasions, they were quick to add that they were holy obsessions, that the Divine Spirit was at work in his rhetoric.

W: What are you driving at? What you are saying is nowhere to be found in his letters or in the Acts.

B: Of course it is, if you labour through his convoluted sentences. His speech before Festus which this listener cut short will have bordered on hysteria.

W: Maybe, or very probably so. This does not give me an idea, however, what you are pursuing now?

B: There are several points I am trying to spread before you. The first is that Paul remained a fanatic through his whole life, to the end, and I cannot stand fanatics. For him the world was a black and white affair. Here, the chosen saints. There, the dark rest of the world which is governed by countless vices, sex in the first line, guilty before God, ruled by the sheitan, doomed for annihilation by fire on the day of reckoning.

(B): Cruel and twisted, it is compounded still by predestination and by not one word, one feeling of pity. On the contrary, a deep satisfaction seems to ooze from the corresponding lines of his letters.

Had it ever occurred to him that love, pity, understanding, mutual help, high moral ethics and social responsibility could be found also in the pagan world, right under his nose, if he cared to realize it? But he did not care and when he stumbled over it he dismissed it probably as a very clever ruse to distract him or his followers from the shining path.

W: I am hearing you out before I answer. What is your second point?

B: The raving Paul was not content to dismiss the dire end of 99% of the world population with a noncomittal shrug, but sent curses after them even in his letters, if you read the end of his first writing to the Corinthians.

Point three: all this would be somehow still rational if he cursed declared enemies of his creed and would triumph over the vengeance that his God - which is the old Jahve again - will exact over the soldiers of evil, but this is not enough for him.

The final holocaust, so he is wishing, should also bring eternal pain for those „who do not know God". Read his letter to the Thessalonians, if you do not believe it!
And here is the point where I am finished with Paul once and for all. This cannot be excused by fanatic or hysterical rhetoric, this is the manifest and monstrous final sin against the Spirit. Of this I accuse him herewith!

W: Easy now, my friend! And hear me out as I did just now.
First of all, we have come in our studies upon many a new religion during the past 5.000 years, around the Mediterranean, Persia, India for instance. Hardly any of them failed to condemn the present and future detractors and non-believers, in terms against which Paul is a paragon of restraint.

B: But -

W: Sorry, I have the floor now. These curses, however, were meant to work far more inward than outward. Inward, to the believers, each curse was a bulwark that fended off attacks or temptations from the new-found belief. The more drastic the curse, the higher the fortifications, because the faithful really believed that their founder, leader, prophet or whatever had the supernatural power to have the curses really work. So Paul, forgetting for a moment that he was preaching Yeshua's teachings gave them the irate, offended, vengeance-brooding Jahve again. I think that this is most unfortunate and hardly in consonance with the Sprit who talked fromYeshua, but it certainly is not a declaration of war against the rest of humanity, as you want to see it.

B: I think that your defense is very weak indeed, sorry! What you are trying to do is to shield the incredible arrogance of Paul behind the famous „historical context", insinuating that his faux pas, as you like to see it, is excusable before the background of curses uttered by Egyptain priests or by Zarathustra.

No, sir! With that you bring relativity also against the teachings from Yeshua who received no better fate by their early administrators and which will presumably end after

(B): some 2.000 years or so in a new version. I am putting it to you with utter clarity: Paul besmirched the revelation through Yeshua with his fanatic ideas on God's vengeance on the rest of the world and he vilified himself also with his curses!

W: „.... he shall throw the first stone ..." Remember? You came here by car. How often did you curse other drivers on the way?

B: Now don't give me this kind of comparison, please, or I quit the discussion! If I call an idiot a damned donkey I am not out for his eternal life, and I have forgotten it in the next minute. He is not my enemy. And one minute later I am the blasted idiot of another driver, male or female, who has forgotten me already after 20 seconds. Sorry, this is no comparison. Have you no better arguments?

W: I don't know. Have you never been consumed by a task that is binding all of your attention, energy, devotion? I am sure you have. In such a state nearly everything else is reduced to a nuisance compared to what you are doing and any disturbance or opposition, be it real or imagined, is dealt with in a vocabulary which you do not use otherwise - and of which you are sorry in the next moment?

B: I see where you are driving at. You are saying that Paul was practically in a state of high tension all the time and was carried away sometimes in his rhetoric, no?

W: This is how I see it.

B: This is how I see it definitely not! It is a great difference for me if somebody is groping for words or is heaping half-baked notions on top of each other which, taken together in the end, are dutifully consumed by the uneducated listeners as higher or highest revelation. But in all this there has to be a basic mainstream of decency underneath which I cannot pinpoint otherwise than by tolerance, pity, love and a preparedness to forgive. Paul did not have this basic decency; what is worse, he did not feel that he should have it.

W: Then of what is Paul guilty in your opinion?

B: He betrayed himself, because he sang the praise of love which we printed in the introduction to our small book. He betrayed his listeners and the future generations of them because they drew for the next 1.900 centuries on his intransigence and lack of the most basic humanitarian values. And he betrayed the revelation through Yeshua, because this has still the central tenet to have understanding, pity, even love on your neighbour. It is a big consolation that even Paul was not able to ruin that teaching.

W: What would you say to Paul if he were standing before you in this moment?

B: He is, I am quite sure. And I am saying to him: „I am not going to curse you. Forgiveness is the word for us all.“

Original texts that have a bearing on Section 11:

Quotation	**Source**
If somebody does not love our Lord Jesus Christ he should be damned.	Cor I, XVI, 22
But though we, or an angel from heaven, preach any other gospel unto you that which we have preached unto you, let him be damned!	Gal I, 9
As we said before, so say I now again: if any man preach any other gospel unto you that you have received, let him be damned!	Gal I, 9
Do you not know that the saints shall judge the world?	Cor I, VI, 2
Don't you know that we shall judge the angels?	Cor I, VI, 3
.... when the Lord Jesus shall be revealed from heaven with his mighty angels, in flaming fire taking vengeance on those who do not know him and are not following of our Lord Jesus Christ	Thess II, I, 8-9

Quotation	Source
Alexander the smith has done me many wrongs; the Lord reward him according to his works. Beware of him! For he has very much resisted our teachings.	Timoth II, IV, 14
For the wrath of God is revealed from heaven over all ungodliness and unrighteousness of men who hold the truth in unjustness	Rom I, 18

12 With all due pity

W: I am starting our last Section squarely with the question:
Does the Divine Spirit speak from Paul's letters?

B: Not in the central issues which we have covered. Besides them there are sometimes evolutionary glimpses, e.g. when he is speaking about the waiting of the creation to come into fullfilment - not of its own, but again harnessed to the glorification of the chosen children of God. Or admitting that we are seeing things now through a glass darkly - but this is about all. Truly evolutionary is nothing of it and he missed sadly in the central issues. Therefore I say: I do not see the Divine Spirit at work in him who spoke through Yeshua and who definitely pointed to other priorities. What is your opinion?

W: The same. What keeps me wondering all the time is that if Paul had not more to offer, or nothing else than what is contained in the letters that we have in hand, how was he ever able to convince thinking and educated people in the Greek and Roman realm? I am not speaking about the simple minds who went for his fiery rhetoric. I am also not talking about the Hebrews-turned-Christians because for them the new High Priest Christ promised some continuity in the traditional lore and law. But how could the others be induced to swallow half of Jewish tribal history and another half of a pattern of behaviour which is not encouraging but twisted and defeatist in its essence?

B: Paul is giving the answer to your question himself: his message is anathema to most Hebrews and a folly to the pagans. In fact, he revels in the frailty of his efforts and is immensely proud of it. Could it be that there is something still hidden in his teachings that has not caught our eye? Were we too arrogant maybe, too prejudiced in order to hear the faint song of evolution below his loud message?

W: I think we can say that we were not arrogant; prejudiced maybe. What we were looking for invain in Paul was the simple joy of having received the revelation which points far above the day, which is also radiating and communicating this joy to the rest of the world, that has tolerance, pity and love as its natural components, but also the will to model and to improve our terrestrial future instead of bowing meekly to a pre-ordained fate.

Moreover the notion that we are not the playballs of evolution but that evolution can be speeded up if this consciousness spreads. Paul in my opinion turned out to be the stern moral theologian of the revelation; he killed joy, he did not allow humour, he was a captive of sexual frustration, he disliked women, hated the body and preached an incredibly boring puritanism - and salvation for the chosen few only! Glad tidings? Liberating message? Holy Spirit? None of it!

B: If there is any supernatural happening in this whole story it is the fact that this belief, with all its joylessness and contradictions, could advance to world importance.

W: There we are at the point, my friend. It was not advanced by planning from above; it could advance only because it was a fanatic movement that pushed into the void left by a pagan state religion that had ceased to be a religion long ago. Only the rites of it were sustaining feudal rule and the spoils of ruthless imperialism. So the movement took hold, inspite of persecution, until the spent state religion crumbled, and not only that, but the whole Roman empire.

And then came the big fourth century for the new faith: Constantine and Theodosius needed new and reliable structures of administration, which the young church and her cadres offered. So she was tolerated first and very quickly made state religion. Supernatural influence? Hardly. It was power engineering, the forming of an unholy coalition that should suppress the progress of mankind in the last essence for centuries to come.

Paul had long before become an authority that nobody dared to question any more. It is a great pity that Peter or Yochanaan were not more productive in their writings. Perhaps they would have formed a corrective influence; I think that Paul stifled their plans, if they had any in this respect, jealously guarding his spiritual fiefdom in the pagan world.

B: So what should the so-called christian churches or sects do about Paul in your opinion? Disclaiming that he wrote in the Holy Spirit? Admitting that they held their believers captive of his notions for more than 1.900 years?

W: This would be about the last thing they would dare to do. Removing the central pillar of their already shaky structure would bring the whole edifice of their commanded faith down in a crash. They could tolerate the end of Paul, but not the end of their organizations.

B: We started our discussions with a Section called „With all due respect“. Are you upholding this respect for Paul now in view of fact what he did to the revelation? And to evolution?

W: It would fall back on anybody, of whatever creed, to say that Paul should not merit personal respect. But the respect I pay to people is not made of one element only, I reserve certain mixtures thereof. I respect Paul's undeniable virtues: full dedication, iron will, enduring torture, dangers, near and final execution. But I do not accord him the status of a „great man“ or „great mind“, because I always hold these attributes over the measuring rod of a contribution toward humanity, enlarging our vision of the place we are living on and of the surrounding cosmos, bringing out the good sides in men and women, nudging along evolution whether they are aware of it or not.

Paul, in my opinion, does not answer to these categories. Therefore I limit my respect to the aforesaid. But I am adding that he deserves also a lot of pity, because he was one of the most torn and unhappy men in history of whom we know.

B: Don't you think that this attitude smells a little bit of condescension, arrogance and holier-than-thou elitism?

W: Not in the least, this be far from me! I meant it honestly and clearly. Perhaps I should say that Paul is entitled to all due pity, very much of it!

B: But he should be shelved for good, no?

W: It would be quite enough if he received another place on the book shelve. With a little humour we place him among the great philosophers, which he so detested without having read them. I think that this is a very fitting and respectful place.

B: And the so-called christian churches and especially the sects which are upholding their literal belief in him?

W: My recommendation is that they should read him once more. And when they come to the lines where he is stating that the letter kills but only the Spirit brings life, they should close the book on him also in respect, forever, and shelve it to its proper place.

B: What is our last line in this book?

W: None, because this whole Section has been one long exit line.
We shall meet, Paul!

On the author

Bert Widman was born in 1934 in Bavaria/Southern Germany. He entered the banking profession and was active in development banking, general contracting and export consulting for some 40 years.

His professional life brought him into early contact with different cultures and religions. This prompted him to take up the study of cultural history and philosophy since three decades, a never-ending and rewarding task in his opinion.

Not belonging to any church or sect he believes in a Creative Spirit which used the man Yeshua as its intermittent mouthpiece. So-called christian churches and sects made - and are still making - a singular travesty of this revelation. Evolution is not allowed to enter, so they end their life cycle as any priest-run organizations have done since 5.000 terrestrial years.

Bert Widman's prime interest is to penetrate beyond their present burial stage. For him, evolution is a universal constant. This is why burnt-out faith organizations, formerly criminal and corrupt, will sink into the abyss of oblivion; not so the misused revelation, however. For her a massive evolutionary metamorphosis is just coming up over the horizon, Mr. Widman maintains.

The author is living in second marriage, has three grown children and four grandchildren and resides near Lake Chiemsee, Bavaria.

Books by Bert Widman :

The Stone Age Of Faith

An evolutionary farewell
to churches and sects.
In plain language.
ISBN 3-89811-204-7

Why, Paul ?

An evolutionary inquiry.
In plain language.
ISBN 3-89811-202-0

Ahead Of Their Times

An evolutionary presentation
of eminent heretics.
In plain language.
ISBN 3-89811-203-9

GEORG LINGENBRINK GMBH & CO. PUBLISHERS
Hamburg Frankfurt